Joseph Edkins

Progressive Lessons in the Chinese Spoken Language

With lists of common words and phrases, and an appendix containing the laws of

tones in the Peking dialect

Joseph Edkins

Progressive Lessons in the Chinese Spoken Language
With lists of common words and phrases, and an appendix containing the laws of tones in the Peking dialect

ISBN/EAN: 9783743407275

Manufactured in Europe, USA, Canada, Australia, Japa

Cover: Foto ©Paul-Georg Meister /pixelio.de

Manufactured and distributed by brebook publishing software (www.brebook.com)

Joseph Edkins

Progressive Lessons in the Chinese Spoken Language

IN THE

CHINESE SPOKEN LANGUAGE;

WITH

LISTS OF COMMON WORDS AND PHRASES,

AND AN APPENDIX CONTAINING THE

LAWS OF TONES IN THE PEKING DIALECT.

BY

JOSEPH EDKINS,

LONDON MISSIONARY SOCIETY.

PEKING.

PREFACE

This little work is intended to assist beginners in the Chinese spoken language. The request has often been made to me, to prepare a simple work in the form of a Vocabulary, as being a want felt by learners. The attempt is here made to supply this want, and to provide a manual which may be suitable for those, who wish to acquire the common phrases of conversation, without attempting to unravel the more subtle intricacies of the language.

In the first part of the work the standard Mandarin orthography has been used. It is found in a printed form in the Wu fang yuen yin 五方元音, a compact and useful native dictionary which may be advantageously consulted for the sounds of words. Farther on, (57th page) I have adopted the peculiarities of the Peking dialect,—which are given with great fulness in Mr. Wade's recent and valuable work "The book of Experiments."

In the Appendix will be found the laws of the Peking dialect in regard to tones, which will be of assistance to those who may be perplexed by incongruities, which are here reduced to something like a system.

All who desire to become really good speakers in this language should study the tones. The knowledge of this peculiarity in Chinese words, lends great distinctness to what is said, and the dryness of the study is much more than compensated, by the pleasure found in being readily understood. The difficulty experienced in distinguishing and learning the tones is much less than is generally supposed.

The tones are marked in this work chiefly according to the standard five-tone system, or that now prevailing at Nanking, and in the northern part of Kiang-su and Ngan-hwei. Such is the system adhered to in the native Mandarin dictionary mentioned above, and by Premare, Morrison, Medhurst, and other authors.

TABLE OF CONTENTS.

Lessons 1 to 52.

Lessons.
1 to 11. Common Words.
12. Boating.
13. The House.
14. Money.
15. The Country.
16. The Body.
17. Conversation.
18. Tailor.
19. Society.
20. Messages.
21. Measures.
22. Worship.
23. Man.
24. Time.
25. Strength and Skill.
26. Mason's work.
27. Study.
28. Ancestors.
29. Servants.
30. Trade.
31. War.
32. Surgery.
33. The Well.
34. Dinner.
35. Arresting a Criminal.
36. Buying Land.
37. Tigers.
38. Elephants.
39. Silver mines.
40. Water.
41. Coals at Peking.
42. Junk Navigation.
43. Furs.   [factures.
44. Imported foreign Manu-
45. Foreign Tribute.
46. Emperor's Seal.
47. Gratitude, an anecdote.
48. Generosity, an anecdote.
49. Self-control, an anecdote.
50. Integrity, an anecdote.
51. Rules for a free School.
52. A Cavern.

Lists of Useful Words and Short Phrases.

1. Place and Direction.
2. Time.
3. Affirmative and Negative Expression.
4. Common Adjectives.
5. Prepositions.
6. Postpositions.
7. Fragmentary Clauses at the end of Sentences.
8. Conjunctions.
9. Names of Imports, Wax,
10. Incense, Pepper, etc. [etc.
11. Medicines.
12. Miscellaneous articles.
13. Marine productions.
14. Dyes and Colours.
15. Woods.
16. Time pieces, Telescopes, [etc.
17. Cotton Goods.
18. Woollens, etc.
19. Metals.
20. Precious Stones, etc.
21. Animal Products.
22. Exports—Oil, Wax, etc.
23. Medicines.
24. Miscellaneous Articles.
25. Colours, Paper, etc.
26. Various Wares.
27. Wood.
28. Clothing.
29. Native Linen and Cotton Manufactures.
30. Silk Manufactures.
31. Articles of Food, etc.
32. Common Utensils.
33. Vegetables.
34. Domestic Animals.
35. Birds.
36. Fishes.
37. Cart Furniture, etc.
38. Words Used in Building.
39. Liquids.

40. Clothing.
41. Sickness.
42. Boat furniture, etc.
43. House furniture.
44. Insects, Reptiles, etc.
45. Common Verbs.
46. Distinctive numeratives.

47. Significant numeratives.
48. Weights and Measures.
49. Collectives.
50. Auxiliary nouns of quali-[ty.
51. Numeral particles to verbs
52. Phrases at an Inn.

APPENDIX.

I. Tones of the Peking dialect.
II. Tones of Nanking dialect.
III. Tones at Chefoo.

Alphabet and Tone marks.

1. The five vowels i, e, a, o, u, when they are not followed by a final n or ng, have the Italian sound. They are the vowels contained in the words fee, fay, papa, foe, too.

2. The vowels i, e, when followed by n or ng, are pronounced as the vowels in fin, and fun. But after i and y, the vowel e is to be sounded as e in sent. A, o, u, when n and ng follow are unaffected by that circumstance.

3. The vowel ĭ is heard like e, in *middle, tassel, ancle.*

4. The vowel ü is heard like u, in the French words *tu, une.*

5. The vowel è is heard as the first e, in *there,* or as ea in *bear.*

6. The mute and sibilant consonants k, t, p, f, s, sh, ch, are pronounced as in English. Though sometimes a little softened in northern dialects, so as to be heard like g, d, b, etc, this need not be noticed in expressing their proper orthography.

7. An inverted comma above the line follows the consonants k, t, p, ts, ch, when they are aspirated. In such cases a strong guttural aspirate closely follows the sound of these consonants. Pronounce the word Tahiti without the vowel a. This might be expressed by T'iti, according to the orthography now explained.

8. In the mandarin of the north and the west, the initials h and s coincide before i and ü. The sound formed by this union may be denominated a sibilant h, or an aspirated s, and the spelling *hs* has been proposed for it, but it will probably become sh in the course of years.

9. In the same dialects, ts and k coincide before the same vowels i and ü. The sound thus formed may be written k, ts, or ch. It is not plainly defined, and is constantly hovering between these various phonetic values. After a further period of change, it will probably determine itself finally into a distinct ch. Every word is pronounced evenly, or with a rising or falling inflection of the voice, or with a double inflection. It may be pitched high or low, according to the usage of any particular dialect, and be enunciated quickly or slowly. All words in the language are arranged in four or five large groups, and one of these tones or inflections is attached to each. Thus the great class to which each word belongs is known, by the intonation with which it is habitually pronounced.

10   The five tone-classes are marked in the following manner:

Tone class.	Chinese name.	Examples.
First tone.	上平 shang pʻing	烏 ˌwu
Second tone.	上聲 shang sheng	五 ʼwu
Third tone.	去聲 cʻhü sheng	務 wuʻ
Fourth tone.	入聲 juh sheng	屋 wuh
Fifth tone.	下平 hia pʻing	無 ˌwu

※※※ For Nanking mandarin, the fourth tone-class or juh sheng is marked with a final h. In the North, the words of this tone-class are distributed among the other tone classes, and the number of tones is then four.

PROGRESSIVE LESSONS

IN THE

CHINESE SPOKEN LANGUAGE.

LESSON 1.

我 'Wo, *I*.
你 'Ni, *thou*.
他 ,T'a, *he*.
人 .Jen, *man*.
樹木 Shu' muh, *trees*.
書 ,Shu, *book*.
這個 Che' ko', *this*.
是 Shï', *is; was*.
的 Tih, *sign of possessive*.

我們 'Wo .men, *we*.
你們 'Ni .men, *you*.
他們 ,T'a .men, *they*.
(船) .C'hwen, *ship; boat*.
絲 ,Sï, *silk*.
水 'Shui, *water*.
那個 Na' ko', *that*.
不 Puh, *not*.
來 .Lai, *come*.

這個人不來 che' ko' .jen puh .lai, *this man did not come*.
我們的船 'wo .men tih .c'hwen, *our ship*.
他們的絲 ,t'a .men tih ,sï, *their silk*.
不是我們的 puh shï' 'wo .men tih, *it is not ours*.
這個書不是你的 che' ko' ,shu puh-shï' 'ni-tih, *this book is not yours*.

LESSON 2.

有 'Yeu, *have; there is*.
沒有 Muh 'yeu, *have not*.
這裏 Che' 'li, *here*.
這樣 Che' yang', *this sort*.

好 'Hau, *good*.
不好 Puh 'hau, *bad*.
那裏 Na' 'li, *there*.
那樣 Na' yang', *that sort*.

在 Tsai‘, at; in; to be at. 都 ,Tu, all.
多 ,To, many. 少 ‘Shau, few.
大 Ta‘, great. 小 ‘Siau, little.
高 ,Kau, high. 低 ,Ti, low.
這個不是好人 che‘ ko‘ puh shi̇̆ ‘hau ,jen, this is not a good man.
好人少 ‘hau ,jen ‘shau, good man are few.
在這裏有水 tsai‘ che‘ ‘li ‘yeu ‘shui, there is water here.
這個絲不好 che‘ ko‘ ,sï puh ‘hau, this is not good silk.
他們都在這裏 ,t‘a ,men ,tu tsai‘ che‘ ‘li, they are all here.
這樣樹木好 che‘-yang‘ ‘shu-muh ‘hau, trees of this sort are good.
這裏的人不少 che‘ ‘li tih ,jen puh ‘shau, the men here are not few.
大書有小書沒有 ta‘ ,shu ‘yeu ‘siau ,shu muh ‘you, there are large books, but no small ones.

LESSON 3.

拿來 .Na .lai, bring. 拿去 .Na k‘ü‘ (c‘hü), take away.
走 ‘Tseu, walk. 去 K‘ü‘, go.
東西 ,Tung ,si, thing. 事情 Shï‘ .t‘sing, a matter.
甚麼 Shen‘ ‘mo, what? 那裏 ‘Na ‘li, where?
叫 Kiau‘, call; is called. 幾時 ‘Ki ,shï, when?
衣服 ,I fuh, clothes. 布 Pu‘, cotton cloth.
綢 ,C‘heu, woven silk; ponge[e]. 瓶 ,P‘ing, bottle; pitcher.
這個綢叫甚麼 che‘ ko‘ .c‘heu kiau‘ shen‘ ‘mo, what is this silk called?
這個是好東西 che‘ ko‘ shï‘ ‘hau ,tung ,si, this is a good thing.
那個瓶不大 na‘ ko‘ .p‘ing puh ta‘, that bottle is not large.
不是我的衣服 puh-shï‘ ‘wo tih ,i fuh, they are not my clothes.
他不去 ,t‘a puh k‘ü‘, he did not go.
拿書來 .na ,shu .lai, bring books.
東西拿去 ,tung ,si .na k‘ü‘, take the things away.
船那裏 .c‘hwen ‘na ‘li, where is the boat?
布幾時拿來 ‘pu‘ ‘ki ,shï .na .lai, when did you bring the cloth?

這樣絲多 che' yang' ,sï ,to, *there is much of this silk* (raw silk.)

那樣樹木不大 na' yang' shu- muh' puh ta', *that kind of tree is not large.*

LESSON 4.

自己 Tsï 'ki, *self*.
全 T'siuen, *all; whole*.
各 Koh, *each; every*.
些 ,Sie, *a few of*.
這些 Che' ,sie, *this sort of*.
向 Hiang', *towards; to*.
說 Shwoh, *to say; speaking*.

這麼樣 Che' 'mo yang', *thus*.
怎麼樣 'Tsen 'mo yang', [*how?*
做 Tso', *do; make*.
和 .Ho, *with; harmony*.
同 .T'ung, *together with*.
從 .T'sung, *from; to accord*.
要 Yau', *to want; beg.* [*with.*

他自己沒有 ,t'a tsï 'ki muh 'you, *he himself has it not.*
我們全去 'wo .men .t'siuen k'ü', *we will all go.*
你去叫他來 'ni c'hü' kian' ,t'a .lai, *go and call him.*
幾時從上海來 'ki .shï .t'sung Shang' 'hai .lai, *when did you come from Shanghai?*
這些人都是廣東來的 che' ,sie ,jen ,tu shï' 'Kwang ,tung .lai tih, *these persons (or persons of this sort) all come from Canton.*
各人自己說 koh ,jen tsï 'ki shwoh, *let each one speak for himself.*
全是這麼樣 .t'siuen shï' che' 'mo yang', *it is all so.*
不做甚麼 puh tso' shen' 'mo, *he does nothing.*
這布怎麼樣做的 che' pu' 'tsen ,'mo yang' tso' tih, *how is this cloth made?*
綢那裏做的 .c'heu 'na 'li tso' tih, *where is woven silk made?*
向他說要衣服 hiang' ,t'a ,shwoh yau' ,i-fuh, *he said to him that he wanted clothes.*

LESSON 5.

給 K'ï ('kei), *give*.
話 Hwa', *language; words*.
呢 .Ni, *final interrogative*.
紅 .Hung, *red*.

了 'Liau, *sign of the past*.
畫 Hwa', *picture; to draw*.
燈 ,Teng, *lamp*.
金 ,Kin, *gold*.

門 .Men, door.
寫 'Sie, to write.
中國 ,Chung kwoh, China.
現在 Hien' tsai', at present.
太陽 T'ai' yang, the sun.
筆 Pih, pencil; pen.
替我 T'i' 'wo, for me.

斤 ,Kin, a catty; 1¼ lbs.
字 Tsï', characters.
外國 Wai' kwoh, foreign.
皇帝 .Hwang ti', emperor.
月亮 Yuèh liang', the moon.
紙 'Chï, paper.
茶葉 .C'ha yèh, tea in leaf.

寫了字呢 'sie 'liau tsï' .ni, have you written?
給他紙用 kih ('kei) ,t'a 'chï yung', give him paper to use.
拿筆來寫字 .na pih .lai 'sie tsï', bring a pencil to write.
有個紅門 'yeu ko' .hung .men, there is a red door.
拿畫來看 .na hwa' .lai k'an', bring pictures for me to see.
現在皇帝好的 hien' tsai' .hwang ti' 'hau tih, the present emperor is good.
沒有月亮 muh 'yeu yuèh liang', there is no moonlight.
太陽太大 t'ai' yang t'ai' ta', the sun is very powerful.
他的衣服紅 t'a tih ,i fuh .hung, his clothes are red.

LESSON 6.

一 Yih, one; a.
二 Rï', two.
三 ,San, three.
四 Sï', four.
五 'Wu, five.
箇 Ko', numeral for men, etc.
買 'Mai, buy.
用 Yung', to use; eat.
能 .Neng, can.
為甚麼 Wei' shen' 'mo, [why?]

六 Luh or lieu', six.
七 T'sih, seven.
八 Pah, eight.
九 'Kieu, nine.
十 Shïh, ten.
本 'Pen, root, numeral for books.
賣 Mai', sell.
用人 Yung' .jen, servant.
穿 C'hwen, to insert; put on.
曉得 'Hiau teh, to know.

七個用人 t'sih ko' yung' .jen, seven servants.
要三四個 yau' ,san sï' ko', I want three or four.
買五斤茶葉 mai' 'wu ,kin .c'ha yèh, buy five catties of tea.
賣紙的人 'mai 'chï tih .jen, a man who sells paper.
穿紅衣服 ,c'hwen .hung ,i fuh, he put on red clothes.

拿三個燈 .na ,san koʻ ,teng, *bring three lamps.*
六個人用茶 luh koʻ ,jen yungʻ .cʻha, *six men took tea.*
買一本書 ʻmai yih-ʼpen ,shu, *buy a book.*
這裏不能買書 cheʻ ʻli puh .neng ʻmai ,shu, *here books cannot be bought.*
為甚麼不去 weiʻ shenʻ ʻmo puh cʻhüʻ, *why do you not go?—*

LESSON 7.

看 Kʻanʻ, *to see.*
查 .Cʻha, *to seek.*
鞋子 .Hiai tsï̌, *shoes.*
洗臉 ʻSi lienʻ, *wash one's face.*
走路 ʼTseu luʻ, *to walk.*
快 Kʻwaiʻ, *sharp; quickly.*
飯 Fanʻ, *rice.*
好 ʻHau, *well; good; done.*
天 ,Tʻien, *heaven; day; wea-*
上 Shangʻ, *above.* [*ther.*

不見 Puh kienʻ, *to lose; lost.*
刷 Shwah, *to brush.*
釘 Ting, *a nail.*
釘 Tingʻ, *to nail.*
慢 Manʻ, *slow; slowly.*
刀 Tau, *knife; sword.*
[soon 吃飯 Cʻhih fanʻ, *take dinner.*
學 Hioh (.hiau), *to learn.*
地 Tïʻ, *earth.*
下 Hiaʻ, *below.*

東西不見了 ,tung, si puh kienʻ ʻliau, *things are lost.*
刷這個衣服 shwah cheʻ koʻ ,i fuh, *brush these clothes.*
釘那個門 tingʻ .na koʻ .men, *nail that door.*
慢慢走 manʻ manʻ ʻtseu, *walk slowly; wait a little.*
走路快 ʼtseu luʻ kʻwaiʻ, *he walks fast.*
洗好你的臉 ʻsi ʻhau ʼni tih lienʻ, *wash your face well.*
不好看 puh ʻhau kʻanʻ, *not good to see.*
刷鞋子 shwah hiai tsï̌, *brush shoes.*
拿快刀來 .na kʻwaiʻ ,tau .lai, *bring a sharp knife.*
他來快了 tʻa .lai kʻwaiʻ ʻliau, *he will come soon.*
沒有學 muh ʻyou hioh, *I have not yet learned.*

LESSON 8.

生意 ,Sheng iʻ, *trade.*
貴 Kweiʻ, *dear; honourable.*
熱 Jĕh, *hot.*

田裏 ,Tʻien ʻli, *in the fields.*
賤 Tsienʻ, *cheap; poor.*
冷 ʻLeng, *cold.*

不要 Puh yau', *I do not want.*
饅頭 .Man .t'eu, *bread.*
事體 Shï' 't'i, *a matter.*
最 Tsui', *very.*
早 ,Tsau, *early.*
今 ,Kin, *now.*
心 ,Sin, *heart; mind.*
黑 Heh (,hei), *black.*
白 Peh (.pai), *white.*
身子 ,Shen 'tsï, *body.*
頂 'Ting, *most.*
兩個 'Liang ko', *two.* [*few.*
有限 'Yeu hien', *not much;*
起 'K'i ('c'hi), *rise; begin.*

貴的不要 Kwei' tih puh yau', *if dear, I do not want it.*
這個頂賤 che' ko' 'ting tsien', *this is the cheapest.*
到田裏去 tau' .t'ien 'li c'hü', *go into the fields.*
你來不早 'ni .lai puh 'tsau, *you have not come early.*
天熱起來 ,t'ien jeh 'c'hi .lai, *the weather is growing hot.*
天冷要穿的 ,t'ien 'leng yau' ,c'hwen tih, *when the weather is cold I shall wear it.*
生意不好 ,sheng i' puh 'hau, *trade is bad.*
人有限 jen 'yeu hien', *there are few men.*
這些人吃饅頭 che' ,sie .jen c'hih .man- t'eu, *these people eat bread.*
黑的多白的少 heh tih ,to peh tih 'shau, *there are many black, but few white.*
兩斤紅茶葉 'liang ,kin .hung .c'ha yeh, *two catties of black tea.*
早些來 'tsau ,sie .lai, *come earlier.*
他不曉得事體 ,t'a puh .hiau teh shï' 't'i, *he does not know matters:—*

LESSON 9.

狠 'Hen, *exceedingly* (initial).
棉花 .Mien ,hwa, *cotton.*
尺 C'hih, *foot.*
幾個 'Ki ko', *how many?*
雙 ,Shwang, *a pair.*
雞 ,Ki, *fowl.*
羊 .Yang, *sheep; goat.*
魚 .Yü, *fish.*
得狠 Teh 'hen, *exceedingly.*
緞子 Twan' 'tsï, *satin.*
寸 T'sun', *inch.*
好多 'Hau ,to, *very many.*
酒 'Tsieu, *wine; spirit.*
吃肉 C'hih juh (jeu), *eat meat.*
猪 ,Chu, *pig.*
打 'Ta, *beat; catch.*

救性命 kieu‘ sing‘ ming‘, *to save life.*

LESSON 12. BOATING.

先生 ,Sien ,sheng, *sir; teach-* 眞 ,Chen, *true.*
話 Hwa‘, *words.* [*er.* 實在 Shïh tsai‘, *truly.*
船主 .C‘hwen ‘chu, *chief boat-* 停 .T‘ing, *to stop.*
碼頭 ’Ma .t‘eu, *jetty.* [*man.* 搖 .Yau, *to scull.*
錨 .Mau, *anchor.* 拋 ,P‘au, *to cast.*
篷 .P‘eng, *sail.* 起 ’C‘hï, *to raise.*
下 Hia‘, *to let fall.* 櫓 ’Lu, *a scull.*
槳 Tsiang‘, *oar; to row.* 順 Shun‘, *favourable.*
開船 ,K‘ai .c‘hwen, *to start.* 向東 Hiang‘ ,tung, *to go east.*
潮水 .C‘hau ’shui, *tide.* 西邊 Si ,pien, *westward.*
南 .Nan, *south.* 北面 Peh mien‘, *northwards.*
修 ,Sieu, *to repair.* 往 ’Wang, *to go.* [*sir?*
先生到那裏 ,sien ,sheng tau‘ ‘na ’li, *where will you go,*
現在拋錨 hien‘ tsai‘ p‘au .mau, *now cast anchor.*
四個人搖船 si‘ ko‘ .jen .yau .c‘hwen, *four men are sculling.*
往東走 ’wang ,tung ’tseu, *go to the eastward.*
向南邊去 hiang‘ .nan ,pien c‘hü‘, *go to the southward.*
快快起篷 k‘wai‘ k‘wai‘ ’c‘hï .p‘eng, *raise the sail quickly.*
快快搖 k‘wai‘ k‘wai‘ .yau, *scull quickly.*
眞是快船 .chen shï‘ k‘wai‘ .c‘hwen, *it is indeed a fast boat.*
潮沒有來 .c‘hau muh ’yeu .lai, *the flood tide has not begun.*
順風呢 shun‘ ,fung .ni, *is the wind fair?*
要修櫓 the scull needs repairing.
船開去了 .c‘hwen ,k‘ai c‘hü‘ ’liau, *the boat has started.*
停船在這裏 .t‘ing .c‘hwen tsai‘ che‘ ’li, *stop the boat here.*
叫船主來 kiau‘ .c‘hwen ‘chu .lai, *call the boatman here.*

LESSON 13. THE HOUSE.

前門 .T‘sien .men, *front door.* 關 ,Kwan, *to shut.*
蓋 Kai‘, *to build.* 玻璃 ,Po .li, *glass.*
客人 K‘eh‘ .jen, *guest.* 窻 ,C‘hwang, *window.*

堂 .T'ang, hall.
書房 .Shu .fang, library.
地板 Ti' 'pan, floor.
樓 .Leu, upper-story.
樓上 .Leu shang', upstairs.
牆 .T'siang, wall.

梯 ,T'i, stairs.
棹 Choh, table.
椅 'I, chair.
床 .C'hwang, bed.
帳子 Chang' 'tsï, curtain.
火爐 'Ho .lu, fire stove.

關玻璃窗 ,kwan ,po .li ,c'hwang, close the glass windows.
在書房裏有的 tsai' ,shu .fang 'li 'yeu tih, it is in the library.
前門不開 .t'sien .men puh ,k'ai, the front door is not open. [wall.
壘一條長牆 (lei) yih .t'iau .c'hang .t'siang, build a long
上邊蓋樓 shang' ,pien kai' .leu, build an upper-story above.
客人坐在堂上 k'eh .jen tso' tsai' .t'ang shang', the guests are sitting in the hall.
樓上沒有空 .leu shang' muh 'yeu k'ung, there is no space upstairs.
客堂沒有地板 k'eh .t'ang muh 'yeu ti' 'pan, the reception hall has no wooden floor.
主人坐南 'chu .jen tso' .nan, the master sits to the southward.

LESSON 14. MONEY.

錢 .T'sien, money; cash.
洋錢 .Yang .t'sien, dollar.
四開 Sï ,k'ai, shilling.
値 Chih, to be worth.
兌換 Tui' hwan', exchange.
賤 Tsien', poor; cheap.

找 'Chau, to make up money.
鷹洋 ,Ying .yang, Mex. dol-
銀子 .Yin 'tsï, silver. [lar.
還 .Hwan, return money.
多少 ,To 'shau, how many?
市上 Shï' shang', in the market.

貴 Kwei', honourable; dear.
漲起來 'Chang 'c'hi .lai, rise higher. (e. g. price of dollars; also of the tide rising.)
街上 ,Kiai shang', in the
太 T'ai', too. [street.
一兩 Yih 'liang, tael; ounce.
錢 .T'sien, mace; 1-10th of an
分 ,Fen, candareen; 1-100th
角 Kioh, tenth of a dollar. [oz. of an oz. or dollar.
兌換洋錢 tui' hwan' ,yang .t'sien, change the dollars.

找你二百個錢 'chau 'ni rï‘ peh ko‘ .t'sien, *I pay you two hundred cash.* [lars ?

多少鷹洋 ,to 'shau ,ying .yang, *how many Mexican dollars?*

市上沒得買 shï‘ shang‘ muh teh 'mai, *none to be bought in the market.*

東西貴得狠 ,tung ,si kwei‘ teh 'hen, *the things are very dear.*

洋價漲起來 .yang kia‘ 'chang 'c'hi .lai, *the price of the dollar is rising.*

還你一兩二錢 .hwan 'ni yih 'liang rï‘ .t'sien, *I return you one tael and two mace.*

三角四分 ,san kioh sï‘ ,fen, *three-tenths and four-hundreds of a dollar; 34 cents.*

銀子現在賤 .yin-tsï hien‘ tsai‘ tsien‘, *at present silver is cheap.*

價錢太貴 kia‘ .t'sien t'ai‘ kwei‘, *the price is too much.*

不值錢 puh chïh .t'sien, *it is not worth anything.*

LESSON 15. THE COUNTRY.

本鄉 'Pen ,hiang, *my village.*
鄉下 ,Hiang hia‘, *in the village.*
村 ,T'sun, *a village.*
風涼 ,Fung .liang, *cool.*
花草 ,Hwa 't'sau, *flowers and grass.*
今年 ,Kin .nien, *this year.*
遊玩 .Yeu wan‘, *walk for pleasure.*
鴨子 Yah 'tsï, *duck.*
看鴨 ,K'an yah, *watch ducks.*
小孩子 'Siau .hai 'tsï, *little boy.*
庄 'Chwang, *cluster of houses; home stead.*
有趣 'Yeu ,t'sü, *pretty.*
到鄉下去 tau‘ ,hiang hia‘ c'hü‘, *go into the country.*

種地 Chung‘ ti‘, *to sow.*
竹 Chuh, *bamboo.*
里 'Li, *Chinese mile.*
三里 ,San 'li, *English mile.*
走遠 'Tseu 'yuen, *walk far.*
歇 Hieh, *to rest.*
不怕 Puh p'a‘, *not fear.*
近路 Kin‘ lu‘, *near road.*
會走 Hwei‘ 'tseu, *can walk.*
辛苦 Sin 'k'u, *tired.*
風水 ,Fung 'shui, *wind and water.*
竹林 Chuh .lin, *bamboo grove.*
刮 Kwah, *to blow.*

鄉下人 ,hiang hia' ,jen, *countryman.*
上街去了 shang' ,kiai shi' c'hü' 'liau, *to go to market.*
看鴨的人 ,k'an yah tih ,jen, *a duck-keeper.*
在鄉下雞多 tsai' ,hiang hia' ,ki ,to, *in the country fowls are numerous.*
走路辛苦 'tseu lu' ,sin 'k'u, *he walked till he was tired.*
三四里路 ,san si' 'li lu', *three or four le.*
村上的百姓 ,t'sun shang' tih peh sing', *the people of the village.*
鄉下小孩子 ,hiang hia' 'siau .hai 'tsi, *village children.*
住在鄉下庄上 chu' tsai' ,hiang hia' ,chwang shang', *he lives in a country hamlet.*
這條路不近 che' .t'iau lu' puh kin', *this road is not near.*
風水狠好 ,fung 'shui 'hen 'hau, *the position is very good.*
刮起風來 kwah 'c'hi ,fung .lai, *it begins to blow.*
不怕路遠 puh p'a' lu' 'yuen, *he does not fear the distance.*
走路快 'tseu lu' k'wai', *he walks quickly.*
花草有趣 ,hwa 't'sau 'yeu ,t'sü, *the flowers are pretty.*
在竹林裏遊玩 tsai' chuh .lin 'li ,yeu wan', *wander for pleasure in bamboo groves.*
沒有風涼的地方 muh 'yeu ,fung .liang tih ti' ,fang, *there is no cool place.*

LESSON 16. THE BODY.

身體 ,Shen 't'i, *the body.*
眼睛 'Yen ,tsing, *eyes.*
瞎 Hiah, *blind.*
斬手 'Chan 'sheu, *cut off the hand.*
頭髮 .T'eu fah, *hair.*
剃 T'i', *shave.*
嘴裏 Tsui' 'li, *in the mouth.*
大脚 Ta' kioh, *large feet.*
胸膛 Hiung .t'ang, *the chest.*
手心 'Sheu ,sin, *palm of hand.*
摸 Moh, *to touch.*

磕頭 K'oh .t'eu, *make a prostration*
帶 Tai', *to carry.*
啣 Hien, *hold in the mouth.*
站 Chan', *stand.*
跑 P'au, *to run.*
餓 Wo', *hungry.*
跳 T'iau', *jump.*
跪拜 Kwei' pai', *kneel and bow.*
心腸 ,Sin .c'hang, *heart.*
躺 ,T'ang, *to lie down.*
生病 ,Sheng ping', *to be sick.*

眼睛瞎了 'yen ,tsing hiah 'liau, *he is blind.*
生了大病 ,sheng 'liau ta' ping', *he has had severe illness.*
跑在路上 .p'au tsai' lu' shang', *running on the road.*
斬了他的頭 'chan 'liau ,t'a tih .t'eu, *they cut off his head.*
站起來 chan' 'c'hi .lai, *stand up.*
躺在床上 ,t'ang tsai' .c'hwang shang', *he is lying in bed.*
帶在手裏 tai' tsai' 'sheu 'li, *carry in the hand.*
手摸一摸看 'sheu moh yih moh k'an', *touch it with your hand and see.* [*very long.*
頭髮不狠長 .t'eu fah puh 'hen .c'hang, *his hair is not*
可以跳下來 'k'o 'i t'iau' hia' .lai, *you can jump down.*
跪下來拜他 kwei' hia' .lai pai' ,t'a, *kneel down and bow to him.*
不要剃頭 puh yau' t'i' .t'eu, *do not shave your head.*
嘴裏啣什麼東西 ,tsui 'li hien shen' 'mo ,tung ,si, *what is he holding in his mouth?*

LESSON 17. CONVERSATION.

貴姓 Kwei' sing', *your name?* 尊 ,Tsun, *honourable.*
名 .Ming, *proper name.* 寒 .Han, *cold; mean; my.*
號 Hau', *literary name.* 處 C'hu', *a place.* [*name?*
貴地 Kwei' ti', *your home?* 高姓 ,Kau sing', *your high*
舍下 She' hia', *my cottage.* 貴庚 Kwei', keng, *your age?*
令 Ling', *honoured; your.* 歲 Sui', *years of age.* [*er.*
敝 Pi', *poor; mean; my.* 令堂 Ling' .t'ang, *your moth-*
令郎 Ling' .lang, *your son.* 寶眷 'Pau ,kiuen, *your wife.*
令愛 Ling' ngai', *your daugh-* 尊駕 ,Tsun ,kia, *you.*
　　　　　[*children.* 　　　　[*ness.*
家眷 ,Kia ,kiuen, *wife and* 貴幹 Kwei', kan, *your busi-*
寶 'Pau, *valuable.* 貴業 Kwei' yeh, *your trade.*
別 Pieh, *other.* 此刻 'T'sï k'eh, *at present.*
位 Wei', *numeral for men.* 現今 Hien', kin, *ditto.*
先生尊姓 ,sien-,sheng ,tsun sing', *teacher, what is your honourable name?*
貴府那裏 Kwei' fu' ,na 'li, *where is your honourable home?*
幾時到敝地 'ki shï tau' pi' ti', *when did you come here?*

貴國是那一國 kwei' kwoh shï' 'na yih kwoh, *of what kingdom are you?* [*year?*
今年貴庚 ,kin .nien kwei' ,keng, *how old are you this*
你來什麽貴幹 'ni .lai shïh 'mo kwei' ,kan, *on what affair have you come?*
令郞幾歲 ling' .lang 'ki sui', *how old is your son?*
寶眷在不在 'pau ,kiuen tsai' puh tsai', *is your wife with you or not?*
別號呢 piĕh hau' .ni, *what is your literary name?*
未有別的說話 muh 'yeu piĕh tih shwoh hwa', *I have nothing more to say.*
此刻來做什麽事 't'sï k'ĕh .lai tso' shïh 'mo sï', *at present what have you come to do?*

LESSON 18. TAILOR.

裁縫 .T'sai .fung, *a tailor.*
針 ,Chen, *needle.*
牢 .Lau, *lasting; strong.*
樣子 Yang' 'tsï, *pattern.*
縫 .Fung, *a seam; to sew.*
大呢 Ta' .ni, *woollen cloth.*
紗 ,Sha, *gauze.*
件 Kien', *numeral for gar-* [ments.
馬掛 'Ma kwa', *jacket.*
長衫 .C'hang ,shan, *long robe.*
短衫 'Twan ,shan, *short coat.*
汗衫 Han' ,shan, *shirt.*
先 ,Sien, *first.*
鈕 'Nieu, *button.* [*work.*
一工 Yih ,kung, *one day's*
鈕口 'Nieu 'k'eu, *button hole.*
袍子 .P'au 'tsï, *thick robe.*
背心 Pei' ,sin, *waist coat.*
剪刀 'Tsien ,tau, *scissors.*
熨 T'ang', *to iron.*
絲線 ,Sï sien', *silk thread.*
綿線 .Mien sien', *cotton thread.*
抵針 'Ti ,chen, *thimble; needle-guard.*
褲子 K'u' 'tsï, *trowsers.*
湖縐 .Hu ,cheu, *crape.*
後來 Heu' .lai, *after.*

做一件長布衫 tso' yih kien' .c'hang pu' ,shan, *make a long cotton robe.* [*side.*
縫在這面 .fung tsai' chĕ' .mien, *place the seam on this*
拿呢裁樣子 .na .ni .t'sai yang' 'tsï, *take the woollen cloth and cut out the pattern.*
用絲線縫的 yung' ,sï sien' .fung tih, *sew it with silk.*
綿線不牢 .mien sien' puh .lau, *cotton thread is not so lasting.*

一件馬掛 yih kien° 'ma kwa°, *one jacket.*
做兩件藍綢衫 tso° 'liang kien° .lan .c'heu ,shan, *make two blue silk gowns.*
先剪樣子 ,sien tsien° yang° 'tsï, *first cut out the pattern.*
做了兩工 tso° 'liau .'liang ,kung, *I have done two day's*
穿起來看 ,c'hwen 'c'hi .lai k'an°, *put it on and see.* [*work.*
大呢裁好了 ta° .ni ,t'sai 'hau 'liau, *the cloth is already cut.*
一條呢褲子 yih .t'iau .ni k'u° 'tsï, *a pair of cloth trowsers.*
鈕扣大小 'nieu 'k'eu t'ai° 'siau, *the button hole is too small.*

LESSON 19. SOCIETY.

朋友 .P'eng 'yeu, *friend.*
老實 'Lau shïh, *honest.*
品行 'P'in hing°, *conduct.*
端方 ,Twan ,fang, *upright.*
挑唆 ,T'iau ,so, *sow discord.*
咱們 'Tsa .men, *we.*
捧見 P'eng° kien°, *to meet.*
荒唐 ,Hwang .t'ang, *lies.*
相與 ,Siang 'ü, *mutually.*
上當 Shang° tang°, *fall into snares.*
認得 Jen° teh, *to know.*
信息 Sin° sih, *news.*

良心 .Liang ,sin, *conscience.*
做官 Tso° ,kwan, *be in office.*
懂得 'Tung teh, *understand.*
老子 'Lau 'tsï, *father.*
娘 .Niang, *mother.*
纔來 .T'sai .lai, *just come.*
長輩 'Chang pei°, *superiors.*
禮貌 'Li mau°, *politeness.*
明白 .Ming peh, *clear ; know.*
請坐 'T'sing tso°, *please sit down.*
走好 'Tseu 'hau, *step carefully.*
晚輩 'Wan pei°, *inferiors.* [*ly.*

不認得這個人 puh jen° teh che° ko° .jen, *I do not know this man.*
不要上當 puh yau° shang° tang°, *do not fall into a snare.*
他上了當 .t'a shang° 'liau tang°, *he is fallen into a snare.*
請坐在這裏 't'sing tso° tsai° che° 'li, *please sit here.*
你是長輩 'ni shï° 'chang pei°, *you are superior.*
我們是晚輩了 'wo .men shï° 'wan pei° 'liau, *we are your inferiors.*
那個朋友不老實 na° ko° .p'eng 'yeu puh 'lau shïh, *that friend was not to be trusted.*
荒唐的話 ,hwang .t'ang tih hwa°, *lying words.*

老子娘過了 'lau 'tsï .niang kwoʻ 'liau, *his father and mother are no more.*
咱們懂得 'tsa .men 'tung teh, *we understand.*
良心不好 .liang ,sin puh 'hau, *his conscience is at fault.*
挑唆別個人 't'iau ,so pièh koʻ .jen, *he sowed discord among others.*
狠有禮貌 'hen 'yeu 'li mauʻ, *he has very much politeness.*
他要做官兒 ,t'a yauʻ tsoʻ ,kwan .rï, *he wishes to be a mandarin.*
一個用人纔來 yih koʻ yungʻ .jen .t'sai .lai, *a servant has just come.*

LESSON 20. MESSAGES.

片紙 P'ienʻ 'chï, *visiting card.* 通報 ,T'ung pauʻ, *announce.*
送客 Sungʻ k'eh, *escort guests.* 告訴 Kauʻ suʻ, *inform.*
拿信 .Na sinʻ, *take a letter.* 脚夫 Kioh ,fu, *a runner.*
帶信 Taiʻ sinʻ, *carry a letter.* 挑担 T'iau 'tan, *carry loads.*
回信 .Hwei sinʻ, *reply to letter.* 差 C'hai, *send* (a person).
條紙 T'iau 'chï, *slip of paper.* 寄 Kiʻ, *send* (letter or parcel).
就來 Tsieuʻ .lai, *come directly.* 走信 'Tseu sinʻ, *travel with letters.*
挑 T'iau, *to carry* (with a yoke). 打聽 'Ta ,t'ing, *inquire.*
擡 .T'ai, *to carry* (of two persons). 信局 Sinʻ küh, *letter office.*
問安 Wenʻ ,ngan, *ask how he is.* 騎馬 .C'hi 'ma, *to ride.*
信船 Sinʻ .c'hwen, *letter boat.* 箱子 ,Siang 'tsï, *chest.*
一包 Yih ,pau, *one parcel.* 禮物 'Li wuh, *presents.*
謝謝 Sieʻ sieʻ, *thanks.* 封 ,Fung, *numeral of letters.*
送片紙去 sungʻ p'ienʻ 'chï c'hüʻ, *take a card and present it.*
送客到船上 sungʻ k'eh tauʻ .c'hwen shangʻ, *escort the visitors to the boat.*
帶信到家裏去 taiʻ sinʻ tauʻ ,kia 'li c'hüʻ, *take a letter to your home.*
走信的拿去 'tseu sinʻ tih .na c'hüʻ, *the postman took it.*
回信不要 .hwei sinʻ puh yauʻ, *no answer is wanted.*
問他安謝謝他 wenʻ ,t'a ,ngan ,sie ,sie ,t'a, *ask how he is and thank him.*
差一個人 ,c'hai yih koʻ .jen, *send a man.*
打聽明白 'ta ,t'ing .ming peh, *inquire fully.*

問你的信息 wen' 'ni tih sin' sih, ask news respecting you.
告訴他就要來 kau' su' ,t'a tsieu' yau' .lai, tell him to come at once. [presents.
兩包禮物 'liang ,pau 'li wuh, two parcels containing
檯四隻茶箱 .t'ai sï' chïh .c'ha ,siang, carry four tea chests.
信船沒有到 sin' .c'hwen muh 'yeu tau', the letter boat has not arrived.
送一封信 sung' yih ,fung sin', take one letter. [horseback.
騎馬快快走 .c'hi 'ma k'wai' k'wai' 'tseu, go quickly on
走進去通報 'tseu tsin' c'hü' ,t'ung pau', go in and announce it. [shoulders.
挑東西去 ,t'iau ,tung ,si c'hü', carry these things on your

LESSON 21. MEASURES.

[piece.
升 ,Sheng, pint measure.
疋 P'ih, 40 feet of cloth; a
米 'Mi, rice.
邊 T'ang', column of characters.
斗 'Teu, ten sheng.
句 Kü', sentence. [hours.
麵粉 .Mien ,fen, flour.
時候 .Shï heu', two English
斛 Huh, five teu.
刻 K'eh, quarter of an hour.
小麥 'Siau meh (mai'), wheat.
月 Yueh, a month.
缸 ,Kang, large earthern water
正月 Cheng' yueh, 1st month.
桶 'T'ung, a cask. [vessel.
滿 'Man, full.
雨水 'Yü .'shui, rain water.
步 Pu', 5 feet (land measure).
空 ,K'ung, empty.
畝 'Meu, 240 square pu'.
甕 Ung', large earthern water
過 Kwo', to pass.
殼 Keu', sufficient. [vessel.
下 Hia', to fall; let fall.
一升米不殼吃 yih ,sheng 'mi puh keu' c'hïh, a pint of rice is not enough for him to eat.
買兩個水缸 'mai 'liang ko' 'shui ,kang, buy two large water vessels.
一個時候 yih ko' .shï heu', one Chinese hour.
一句不說 yih kü' puh shwoh, he did not utter a sentence.
一句話不殼 yih kü' hwa' puh keu', one sentence is not enough. [four hours.
過了兩個時候 kwo' 'liau 'liang ko' .shï heu', after

不滿一個月 puh 'man yih ko' yuèh, *not a full month.*
四隻空箱 sï' chïh ,k'ung ,siang, *four empty trunks.*
不過四斤 puh kwo' sï' ,kin, *not more than four catties.*
二百四十步一畝 .rï peh sï' shïh pu' yih 'meu, *240 square pu make one meu.* [*piece.*
四十尺一疋 sï' shïh c'hïh yih p'ih, *forty feet make one*
十寸一尺 shïh t'sun' yih c'hïh, *ten inches one foot.*
十尺一丈 shïh c'hïh yih chang', *ten feet one* chang.
空三兩天 ,k'ung ,san 'liang ,t'ien, *at leisure for two or three days.*
拿一桶酒 .na yih 't'ung 'tsieu, *bring a cask of wine.*
正月裏不空 cheng' yuèh 'li puh ,k'ung, *not at leisure in the first month.*
寫兩遍字 'sie 'liang t'ang' tsï', *write a few columns of characters.*
一刻工夫 yih k'eh ,kung ,fu, *a quarter of an hour's work.*
下了雨不少 hia'.'liau 'ü puh 'shau, *a good deal of rain*
在水綱裏 tsai' 'shui ,kang .'li, *in the water tubs.* [*fell.*
滿到一尺多高 'man tau' yih c'hïh ,to ,kau, *filled to more than a foot high.*

LESSON 22. WORSHIP.

拜 Pai', *to worship.*
神道 .Shen tau', *gods* (Tst.)
神明 .Shen .ming, *ditto.*
佛 Fuh, *Buddha; Buddhas.*
菩薩 ,P'u sah, *Buddhist deities* (2nd class).
羅漢 .Lo han', *do.* (3rd class).
寺院 Shï' yuen', *Buddhist monasteries.* [*priest.*
和尚 .Ho shang', *Buddhist*
功德 ,Kung teh, *merit.*
燒香 ,Shau ,hiang, *burn incense.*
燒紙 ,Shau 'chï, *burn paper.*

上帝 Shang' ti', *God.*
玉帝 Yüh ti', *god of the Tauists.*
廟宇 Miau' 'yü, *Tauist temples.*
籤 ,T'sien, *bamboo divining rods.*
求籤 K'ieu' ,t'sien, *to divine.*
心神 ,Sin .shen, *soul.*
求雨 K'ieu 'ü, *pray for rain.*
財神 .T'sai .shen, *god of riches.* [*ones* (Tauist).
三清 ,San ,t'sing, *three pure*
道士 Tau' shï', *Tauist priest.*
三寶 ,San 'pau, *three precious ones* (Buddhist). [*ers.*
念經 Nien' ,king, *chant pray-*

佛教 Fuh kiau‘, *Buddhist* 添上 ,T'ien shang‘, *to add.*
religion.
面前 Mien‘ .t'sien, *before.* 觀音 ,Kwan ,yin, *goddess of*
百姓 Peh sing‘, *the people.* 婦女 Fu‘ 'nü, *women.* [*mercy.*
這裏百姓拜佛的多 che‘ 'li peh‘ sing‘ pai‘ Fuh tih ,to, *the people here mostly worship Buddha.*
菩薩面前燒香 .p‘u sah mien‘ t'sien ,shau ,hiang, *burn incense before Bu sah.*
廟宇裏去 miau‘ ’ü 'li c‘hü‘, *to go into the temples.*
有事情求籤 ’yeu sï‘ .t'sing .k‘ieu ,t'sien, *if anything has happened inquire of the gods by divination.*
拜財神的多 pai‘ .t'sai .shen tih ,to, *those who worship the god of riches are many.*
佛教有三寶 fuh kiau‘ ’yeu ,san ’pau, *the Buddhist religion has the Three precious ones.*
道教有三清 tau‘ kiau‘ ’yeu ,san ,t'sing, *the Tauist religion has the Three pure ones.*
羅漢有十八個 .lo han‘ ’yeu shïh pah ko‘, *there are eighteen Lohans.*
先有十六個外國人 ,sien ’yeu shïh luh ko‘ wai‘ kwoh .jen, *at first there were sixteen foreigners.*
後來有兩個中國人添上 heu‘ .lai ’yeu ’liang ko‘ ,chung kwoh .jen ,t'ien shang‘, *and afterwards two Chinese were added.*
和尙住在寺院裏 .ho shang‘ chu‘ tsai‘ shï‘ yuen‘ ’li, *Buddhist priests live in their monasteries.*
燒紙拜死人 ,shau ’chï pai‘ ’sï .jen, *burn paper to worship the dead.* [*not rain.*
不下雨的時候 puh hia‘ ’ü tih .shï heu‘, *when it does*
官府上廟求雨 ,kwan ,fu shang‘ miau‘ .k‘ieu ’ü, *the mandarins visit the temples to pray for rain.*

LESSON 23. MAN.

肉身 Juh ,shen, *the body.* 能够 .Neng keu‘, *can.*
靈魂 .Ling .hwen, *the soul.* 復活 Fuh hwoh, *live again.*
永遠 ’Yung ’yuen, *eternal.* 復生 Fuh ,seng, *live again.*

生出來 ,Seng c'huh .lai, *born.*
長壽 .C'hang sheu', *old age.* [*ous.*
爲善 .Wei shan', *to be virtu-*
生病 ,Seng p'ing', *to be sick.*
出世 C'huh shï', *born into the world.*
醫不來 ,E puh .lai, *incur-* [*able.*
本分 'Pen fen', *duties.*
從小 .T'sung 'siau, *from a boy.* [*man.*
得救 Teh kieu', *be saved.*
老人家 'Lau jen ,kia, *old.*
耶穌 .Ye ,su, *Jesus.*
差不多 ,C'ha puh ,to, *about; nearly.*
贖罪 Shuh tsui', *redeem from sin.* [*heaven.*
性命 Sing' ming', *life.*
上天 Shang', t'ien, *ascend to*
教 Kiau', *to cause.* [*honest.*
悔改 'Hwei 'kai, *repent.*
忠厚 Chung heu', *faithful and*
相信 ,Siang sin', *believe.*
肯 'K'eng' *willing.*
總要 "T'sung yau', *you must.*
肉死總要死 juh ,shen 'tsung yau' 'sï, *the body must die.*
靈魂不死 .ling .hwen puh 'sï, *the soul does not die.*
活到永遠 hwoh tau' 'yung 'yuen, *live forever.*
人出世的後來 .jen c'huh shï' tih heu' .lai, *men from their entrance into the world and after.*
全是有罪 .t'siuen shï' 'yeu tsui', *all have sin.*
死了後復活 'sï 'liau heu' fuh hwoh, *to rise again after death.*
耶穌贖罪 .Ye ,su shuh tsui', *Jesus redeems from sin.*
罪是耶穌贖的 tsui' shï' .Ye ,su shuh tih, *sin is ransomed by Jesus.*
不肯相信 puh 'k'eng ,siang sin', *not willing to believe.*
好人上天 'hau ,jen shang', t'ien, *good men ascend to heaven.*
病醫不來 p'ing' ,i puh .lai, *the disease cannot be cured.*

LESSON 24. TIME.

明天 .Ming ,t'ien, *to-morrow.*
常 .C'hang, *constant.*
後天 Heu', t'ien, *day after do.*
又 Yeu', *another; again.*
昨天 Tsoh ,t'ien, *yesterday.*
到過 Tau' kwo', *having gone.*
上晝 Shang' cheu', *forenoon.*
幾會 'Ki hwei', *how often?*
下晝 Hia' cheu', *afternoon.*
來年 .Lai .nien, *next year.*
有時 'Yeu .shï, *sometimes.*
一次 Yih t'sï', *once.*
一會 Yih hwei', *once.*
如今 Ju ,kin, *at present.*

隔 Keh, *to separate; after.*
改日 'Kai jïh, *another day.*
再 Tsai‘, *again.*
難得 .Nan teh, *seldom.*
前日 .T‘sien jïh, *day before yesterday.*

即刻 Tsih k‘eh, *at once.*
從前 .T‘sung .t‘sien, *former-* [ly.
古人 'Ku .jen, *ancient men.*
初 ,C‘hu, *for the first time.*
先到 ,Sien tau‘, *first come.*

他前日子不來 ,t‘a .t‘sien jïh 'tsï puh .lai, *the day before yesterday he did not come.* [gone?
去了幾會 c‘hü 'liau 'ki hwei‘, *how many times has he*
從前有這個事情 .t‘sung .t‘sien 'yeu che‘ ko‘ sï‘ .t‘sing, *formerly there happened this circumstance.*
古人有一句話 'ku .jen 'yeu yih kü‘ hwa‘, *the ancients have a sentence.*
昨天死了 tsoh ,t‘ien 'sï 'liau, *he died yesterday.*
此刻綢緞賤的 't‘sï k‘eh .c‘heu twan‘ tsien‘ tih, *at present silks and satins are cheap.*
為善的難得見 .wei shan‘ tih .nan teh kien‘, *the virtuous are seldom to be met with.*
初到那裏認得 ,c‘hu tau‘ 'na 'li jen‘ teh, *on first arrival how could I know him?*
我們先到 'wo .men sien‘ tau‘, *we arrived first.* [again.
昨天又來了 tsoh ,t‘ien yeu‘ .lai 'liau, *yesterday he came*
常做的 .c‘hang tso‘ tih, *he constantly does it.*
隔一日去一會 keh yih jïh c‘hü‘ yih hwei‘, *go once every other day.*

LESSON 25. STRENGTH AND SKILL.

聰明 ,T‘sung .ming, *intelligent.*
能幹 Neng kan‘, *power.*
才能 .T‘sai .neng, *ability.*
會 Hwei‘, *can (acquired power).*
能 .Neng, *can (natural power).*
可以 'K‘o 'i, *you may.*
靈巧 Ling 'c‘hiau, *ingenious.*
不靈 Puh .ling, *inefficacious.*
聽不出 ,T‘ing puh c‘huh, *I do not hear.*

武藝 'Wu i‘, *military arts.*
手藝 'Sheu i‘, *handicraft.*
手段 'Sheu twan‘, *ditto.*
技藝 'K‘i i‘, *ingenious arts.*
玲瓏 .Ling .lung, *clever.*
隔外 Keh wai‘, *extraordinary.*
希奇 ,Hi .k‘i, *wonderful.*
本事 'Pen shï‘ (sï), *ability.*
氣力 C‘hi‘ lih, *strength.*

聽不來 ,T'ing puh .lai, *I* 呆怹 .Ngai pen', *stupid.*
cannot hear. [see. 管 'Kwan, *to manage.*
看得來 K'an' teh .lai, *I can* 輭弱 'Jwan joh, *feeble.*
朶耳聽不來 'rĭ 'to ,t'ing puh .lai, *I cannot hear* [lit.
my ears cannot hear.
沒有本事做官 muh 'yeu 'pen sĭ' tso' ,kwan, *he has
not the ability to be a mandarin.*
這苦難不能救 che' 'k'u nan' puh .neng kieu', *this
misery cannot be relieved.*
神道拜他不靈 .shen tau' pai' ,t'a puh .ling, *the gods
if you worship them are inefficacious.* [*city.*
不能進城 puh .neng tsin' .c'heng, *you cannot enter the*
不會寫字 puh hwei' 'sie tsĭ', *he cannot write.*
他們隔外的靈巧 ,t'a .men keh wai' tih .ling 'c'hiau,
they are extraordinarily clever.
我是手藝人 'wo shĭ' 'sheu i' .jen, *I am a handicrafts-
man.*
呆怹的人做不來玲瓏的工夫 .ngai pen' tih .jen
tso' puh .lai .ling .lung tih ,kung ,fu, *stupid persons cannot do ingenious work.*
氣力有限沒有武藝 c'hi' lih 'yeu .hien muh 'yeu
'wu i', *his strength is not great, and he has no military
accomplishments.*

LESSON 26. MASON'S WORK.

甎 ,Chwen, *bricks.* [*bricks.* 屋頂 Uh 'ting, *top of house.*
方甎 ,Fang ,chwen, *square* 屋基 Uh ,ki, *foundation.*
瓦 'Wa, *burnt-tiles.* 條 .T'iau, *numeral of length.*
泥 .Ni, *earth; morter.* [*son.* 橫梁 Hung .liang, *cross bms.*
泥瓦匠 .Ni 'wa tsiang', *ma-* 石灰 Shĭh ,hwei, *lime.*
石作 Shĭh tsoh, *stone-mason.* 泥刀 .Ni ,tau, *trowel.*
三層 ,San .t'seng, *three sto-* 量 Liang', *to measure.* [*short.*
橋 .K'iau, *bridge.* [*ries.* 長短 .C'hang 'twan, *long;*
環 .Hwan, *arch.* [*arch.* 寬窄 ,K'wan tseh, *broad;*
牌樓 .P'ai .leu, *memorial* 深 .Shen, *deep.* [*narrow.*
起屋 'C'hi uh, *to build a* 商量 ,Shang liang', *to con-*
house. *sider about.*

甎瓦沒有買來 ,chwen 'wa muh 'yeu 'mai .lai, *the bricks and tiles are not yet bought and brought home.*

叫一個泥瓦匠來 kiau' yih ko' .ni 'wa tsiang' .lai, *call a mason.* [*building a house.*]

商量蓋房屋 ,shang liang' kai' .fang uh, *confer about*

要蓋二層樓 yau' kai' .rï .t'seng .leu, *I want to build two stories above the ground floor.* [*three arches.*]

五十三環橋 'wu shïh ,san .hwan .c'hiau, *bridge of fifty*

蓋屋頂用多少瓦 kai' uh 'ting yung', to 'shau 'wa, *in covering in the roof how many tiles shall you use?*

牌樓多都是敬重女人的 p'ai .leu, to ,tu shï' king' chung' 'nü .jen tih, *there are a great many memorial arches which are all in honour of women.*

量量看多少長短 liang' liang' k'an', to 'shau .c'hang 'twan, *measure it to see how long it is.*

拿泥刀多擺石灰 .na .ni ,tau, to 'pai shïh ,hwei, *take the trowel and put on more lime.*

橫梁長一丈半 .hung .liang .c'hang yih chang' pan', *the cross beams fifteen feet long.*

寬窄嗎一尺寬 ,k'wan tseh ('chai) 'ma yih c'hïh ,k'wan, *as to width let them be a foot wide.*

LESSON 27. STUDY.

讀書 Tuh ,shu, *to study.*
本 'Pen, *numeral of books.*
筆墨 Pih meh, *pens and ink.*
文墨 .Wen meh, *style.*
清爽 ,T'sing 'shwang, *clear.*
文理 .Wen 'li, *book style.*
文章 .Wen ,chang, *essays.*
發達 Fah tah, *rise in life:* [*gent.*
用功 Yung' ,kung, *be dili-*
懶惰 'Lan tu', *lazy.*
偷閒 ,T'eu .hien, *waste time.*
解說 'Kiai shwoh, *explanation.*

方字 ,Fang tsï', *square letters.*
四書 Sï' ,shu, *Four books.*
五經 'Wu ,king, *Five classics.*
孝經 Hiau' ,king, *Book of filial piety.* [*character classic.*
三字經 ,San tsï' ,king, *Three*
小說 'Siau shwoh, *novels.*
幾卷 'Ki kiuen', *how many* [*book.*
開卷 ,K'ai kiuen', *open a*
多看 ,To k'an', *read much.*
益處 Yih c'hu', *benefit.*
教書 Kiau' ,shu, *teach.*

註解 Chu' 'kiai, *commentary.* 開書 .Hien ,shu, *light books.*

要緊 Yau' 'kin, *important.* 也 'Ye, *also.* [man.

不是讀書人 puh shï' tuh ,shu ,jen, *he is not a literary*

用功可以發達 yung' ,kung 'k'o 'i fah tah, *if you are diligent you will rise in life.*

書裏的話叫文理 ,shu 'li tih hwa' kiau' .wen 'li, *phrases used in books are called* wen li.

書要多看 ,shu yau' ,to k'an', *books must be much read.*

在老家教書 tsai' 'lau ,kia kiau' ,shu, *he keeps a school at his own home.*

不多看沒有益處 puh ,to k'an' muh 'yeu yih c'hu', *if you do not read much, it will be of no use.*

先讀四書 ,sien tuh sï' ,shu, *first study the Four books.*

後來看五經 heu' .lai k'an' 'wu ,king, *and afterwards read the Five classics.*

閒書小說不好看 .hien ,shu 'siau shwoh puh 'hau k'an', *light literature and novels are not good to read.*

教小孩子 kiau' 'siau .hai tsï', *in teaching boys.*

先要用方字 ,sien yau' yung' ,fang tsï', *you must first use characters written on squares of red paper.*

這本書幾卷 che' 'pen ,shu 'ki kiuen', *how many chapters does this book contain?* [essays.

不會做文章 puh hwei' tso' .wen ,chang, *he cannot write*

也是要緊的書 'ye shï' yau' 'kin tih ,shu, *this is also an important book.*

LESSON 28. ANCESTORS.

爺 .Ye, *father.*
祖父 'Tsu fu', *grand-father.*
曾祖 ,Tseng 'tsu, *great* ditto.
在上 Tsai' shang', *farther back.* [4th degree.
高祖 ,Kau 'tsu, *ancestor of*
根本 ,Ken 'pen, *root.*
傳下 .C'huen hia', *deliver down.*
孝子 Hiau' 'tsï, *filial son.*

葬埋 Tsang' .mai, *bury.*
入土 Juh 't'u, *enter the ground.*
忘記 .Wang ki', *forget.*
虔誠 .C'hien .c'heng, *reverential.* [of.
照應 Chau' ying', *take care*
掃 'San, *sweep.*
祠堂 Sï' .t'ang, *ancestral temple.*
名字 .Ming tsï', *name.*

棺槨 Kwan kwoh, *coffin & case.* 再題 Tsai' ,t'i, *use again.*
做墳 Tso' .fen, *make a grave.* 祖宗 'Tsu ,tsung, *ancestors.*
子孫 'Tsï ,sun, *posterity.* 祭 Tsi', *to sacrifice.*
祖宗是根本 'tsu ,tsung shï' ,ken 'pen, *ancestors are the root from which men come.*
人全是祖宗傳下來 .jen .t'siuen shï' 'tsu ,tsung .c'huen hia' .lai, *men all spring from the stock of their ancestors.*
祭祖宗到三代 tsi' 'tsu 'tsung tau' ,san tai', *sacrifice to ancestors to the third generation.*
爻母祖爻曾爻高祖祭的多 fu' ,'mu ,'tsu fu' ,,tseng fu' ,,kau 'tsu, tsi' tih ,to, *parents, grand-father, great grand-father, and great great grand-father are sacrificed to by many.*
不做棺槨 puh tso' ,kwan kwoh, *he did not provide a coffin.*
不是孝子 puh shï' hiau' 'tsï, *he is not a filial son.*
上輩的名字 shang' ,pei tih .ming tsï', *the names of elders (in the ancestorial line).* [ployed.
不可以再題 puh 'k'o 'i tsai' .t'i, *should not be again em-*
姓李的祠堂 sing' 'li tih .sï .t'ang, *ancestral temple of the Li family.* [*of flowers.*
那一樣的花草 'na yih yaug' tih ,hwa 't'sau, *which sort*
不從根本上生出來 puh .t'sung ,ken 'pen shang' ,sheng c'huh .lai, *is not produced from a root?*

LESSON 29.　SERVANTS.

相幫 ,Siang ,pang, *assist.* 動氣 Tung' c'hi', *to be angry.*
便喚 Shï' hwan', *employ men.* 耽悞 ,Tan wu', *injury by delay.*
喫飽 C'hïh 'pau, *eat enough.* 小娃子 'Siau ,wa 'tsï, *girl.*
餓死 Ngo' 'sï, *starve.* 不得 Puh teh, *must not.*
凍死 Tung' 'sï, *freeze to death.* 騙 P'ien', *to cheat.*
家主 ,Kia ,chu, *master of* 東家 ,Tung ,kia, *master.*
family.
做飯 Tso' fan', *to cook.* 開消 ,K'ai ,siau, *expend.*
菜飯 T'sai' fan', *vegetables* 看房子 ,K'an .fang 'tsï, *take*
and rice. [cal. *care of a house.*
省儉 'Sheng kien', *economi-* 收拾 ,Sheu shèh, *gather up.*
乾淨 ,Kan tsing', *clean.* 小厮 'Siau ,sï, *waiting boy.*

齊整 .T'si 'cheng, *orderly.*　留心 .Lieu,sin,*apply the mind.*
完 .Wan, *finished.*　照應 Chau' ying', *take care of.*
東西都要乾淨 ,tung ,si ,tu yau' ,kan tsing', *everything must be clean.*
使喚的人不少一百 shï' hwan' tih .jen puh 'shau yih peh, *the number of servants employed is not less than a hundred.*　　　　　　　　　　　　[*is not yet done.*
工夫沒有做完 ,kung fu' muh 'yeu tso' .wan, *the work*
兩個小厮看房子 'liang ko' 'siau ,sï ,k'an .fang 'tsï, *two waiting boys kept the house.*
家主好心 ,kia 'chu 'hau ,sin, *the master is well disposed.*
照應照應他們 chau' ying' chau' ying' ,t'a .men, *he takes care of them.*　　　　　　　　　　[*them to be frozen.*
不教他凍死 puh kiau' ,t'a tung' 'sï, *he will not allow*
也不教他餓死 'ye puh kiau' ,t'a ngo' 'sï, *nor to be starved.*　　　　　　　　　　　　　　　　　[*me.*
你不得騙我 'ni puh teh p'ien' 'wo, *you must not cheat*
東西不留心 ,tung ,si puh .lieu ,sin, *you do not take care of things.*
不在時候上做 puh tsai' .shï heu' shang' tso', *you do not do things at the proper time.*　　　　[*master.*
就悮了東家 ,tan wu' 'liau ,tung ,kia, *you injure your*
總要齊整 'tsung yau' .t'si cheng', (*they*) *must be put in order.*

LESSON 30.　TRADE.

筭盤 Swan' .p'an, *abacus.*　便宜 .P'ien .i, *cheap.* [*house.*
清楚 ,T'sing 'c'hu, *distinct.*　茶棧 .C'ha chan', *tea ware-*
細筭 Si' swan', *carefully reckn.* 櫃 Kwei', *counter.*　[*man.*
筭賬 Swan' chang', *calculate.* 當櫃的 ,Tang kwei' tih, *shop-*
開店 ,K'ai tien', *open a shop.* 失本 Shïh 'pen, *lose capital.*
夥計 'Ho ki', *assistant.*　叨光 ,T'au ,kwang, *beg fa-vour.* [*Shanghae sycee.*
　　　　　　　[*& weights.*
斗秤 'Teu c'heng', *measures* 九八銀 'Kieu pah .yin,
本錢 'Pen .t'sien, *capital.*　碼頭 'Ma .t'eu, *port; jetty.*
利錢 Li' .t'sien, *interest.*　海關 'Hai ,kwan, *custom-house.*　　　　　　　　　　　　　　[*tom.*
公平 ,Kung .p'ing, *just,*　完稅 .Wan shui', *pay cus-*

不對 Puh tui', *not agree.*　數目 Su' muh, *numbers.*
數目不對 su' muh puh tui', *the numbers does not agree.*
秤的斤兩不對 c'heng' tih ,kin 'liang puh tui', *the weight in catties and ounces does not agree.*
筭得不清 swan' teh puh ,t'sing, *it is not clearly calculated.*
開店生意不大 ,k'ai tien' ,sheng i' puh ta', *when he opened shop, his trade was small.*
當櫃的說叨光 ,tang kwei' tih shwoh ,t'au ,kwang, *the shopman said, may I beg custom.*
還他二萬八九銀 .hwan ,t'a rï wan' pah 'kieu .yin, *pay him twenty thousand Shanghae taels.*
沒有本錢 muh 'yeu 'pen .t'sien, *he has no capital.*
城裏茶棧多 .c'heng 'li .c'ha chan' ,to, *the tea warehouses in the city are numerous.*
夥計不老實 'ho ki' puh 'lau shïh, *the assistants are dishonest.*

LESSON 31.　WAR.

兵丁 ,Ping ,ting, *soldier.*　搶奪 'T'siang toh, *rob & plunder.*
官兵 ,Kwan ,ping, *ditto.*　浮橋 Fu .c'hiau, *floating bridge.*
得勝 Teh sheng', *conquer.*　安民 ,Ngan .min, *pacify people.*
贏了 .Ying 'liau, *won.*　投河 T'eu .ho, *leap into a river.*
輸 ,Shu, *defeated.*　投井 T'eu 'tsing, *leap into a well.*
打仗 'Ta chang', *to fight.*　死屍 'Sï ,shï, *corpses.*
敗仗 Pai' chang', *defeat.*　隊伍 Tui' 'wu, *rank and file.*
圍困 .Wei k'wen', *besiege.*　規矩 ,Kwei 'kü, *orderly conduct.*
領兵 'Ling ,ping, *lead soldiers.*　埋伏 .Mai fuh, *ambush.*
放火 Fang' 'ho, *set on fire.*　看更 K'an' ,keng, *keep watch.*
擄會 'Lu .jen, *seize men.*　口號 'K'eu hau', *watchword.*
拉人 ,La .jen, *drag away men.*　砲臺 P'au' .t'ai, *battery.*
守 ,Sheu, *to keep.*　放砲 Fang' p'au', *fire cannon.*
官兵守城 ,kwan ,ping ,sheu .c'heng, *mandarin soldiers keep the city.*
打了一個敗仗 'ta 'liau yih ko' pai' chang', *they fought an unsuccessful battle.*
不會得勝 puh hwei' teh sheng', *they cannot conquer.*

前兩天贏了 .t'sien 'liang ,t'ien .ying 'liau, *two days since they gained a victory.* - [*not strong.*
城頭不堅固 .c'heng .t'eu puh ,kien ku', *the city wall is*
男人投了河 .nan .jen .t'eu 'liau .ho, *the men leaped into the rivers.* [*themselves into the wells.*
女人投了井 'nü .jen .t'eu 'liau 'tsing, *the women threw*
做浮橋過去 tso' .fu .c'hiau kwo' c'hü', *they made a floating bridge to pass by.* [*as captives.*
要擄人去的 yau' 'lu .jen c'hü' tih, *they carry away men*
不守隊伍 puh ,sheu tui' 'wu, *they do not keep rank.*
領了三萬兵 'ling 'liau ,san wan' ,ping, *he marched at the head of thirty thousand soldiers.*
不許搶奪 puh 'hü 't'siang toh, *robbery is forbidden.* [*night.*
今夜的口號 ,kin ye' tih 'k'eu hau', *the pass-word for to-*

LESSON 32. SURGERY.

名聲 .Ming ,sheng, *reputation.* 射傷 She' ,shang, *wound.*
名醫 .Ming ,i, *famed surgeon.* 弩箭 'Nu tsien', *cross-bow* [*ly.* *arrow.* [*vegetable.*)
忽然 Hwuh .jan, *unexpected-* 烏頭 ,Wu .t'eu, (*name of a*
漢朝 .Han .c'hau, *Han dynasty.* 毒藥 Tuh yoh, *poison.*
華陀 .Hwa to', (*a noted sur-* 大盆 Ta' .p'en, *large bason.*
臂 Pi', *arm.* [*geon.*) 接血 Tsieh hiueh, *receive blood.*
帳房 Chang' ,fang, *tent.* [*arm.* 怕痛 P'a' t'ung', *fear pain.*
伸臂 Shen pi', *stretch out the* 割開 Koh ,k'ai, *cut open.*
疼 ,T'eng, *pain.* [*der.* 皮肉 .P'i juh, *skin and flesh.*
袒下 ,T'an hia', *bare the shoul-* 一直 Yih ch'ih, *straight.*
血管 Hiueh 'kwan, *blood-vessel.* 帖 T'ieh, *to stick.*
關夫子 ,Kwan ,fu 'tsï, (*the* 膏藥 ,Kau yoh, *plaister.*
god of war, Kwan yün chang.)
漢朝有關夫子 han' .c'hau 'yeu ,kwan ,fu 'tsï, *in the Han dynasty there was Kwan fu tsï, the god of war.*
被那弩箭射傷了 pei' na' .nu tsien' she' ,shang 'liau, *he was wounded by a cross-bow arrow.*
忽然一個人來告訴 hwuh .jan yih ko' .jen .lai kau' su', *at an unexpected moment, there came a man to say.*—

名醫華陀纔來了 .ming ,i .hwa to' .ts'ai .lai 'liau, *the celebrated surgeon Hwa-to had just arrived.*
請他進帳房來 't'sing ,t'a tsin' c'hang' .fang .lai, *he was invited to enter the tent.*
傷裏有烏頭藥 ,shang 'li 'yeu ,wu .t'eu yoh, *in the wound there was a vegetable poison called Wu t'eu.*
一直到骨頭那裏 yih chïh tau' kuh .t'eu na' 'li, *straight into the bone.*
不是早醫 puh shï' 'tsau ,i, *if not cured early.*
這個臂沒有用 che' ko' pi' muh 'yeu .yung, *the arm would be of no use.*
手裏拿刀 'shen 'li .na ,tau, *in his hand he held a knife.*
大盆在臂底下接血 ta' .p'en .tsai pi' ti' hia' tsiëh hiuëh, *a large bason under the arm to catch blood.*
關夫子伸手 kwan ,fu 'tsï ,shen 'shen, *the god of war held out his arm.*   [clothing.
袒下衣服 't'an hia' ,i fuh, *and bared his shoulder of*
教華陀割開 kiau' .Hwa to' koh ,k'ai, *for Hwa-to to cut it open.*
一點不怕痛 yih 'tien puh p'a' t'eng', *he did not in the least fear pain.*
把刀向骨頭上刮去毒氣 'pa ,tau hiang' kuh .t'eu shang' kwah c'hü' tuh c'hi', *he took the knife and approaching the bone scratched away the poison.*
後來皮肉縫起來 heu' .lai .p'i juh .fung 'c'hi .lai, *afterwards the skin and flesh were sewn up.*   [much.
關夫子大笑 ,Kwan ,fu 'tsï ta' sian', *Kwan fu tsï laughed*
說說閒話 shwoh shwoh .hien hwa', *and talked on ordinary subjects.*

LESSON 33. THE WELL.

座 Tso', *numeral of wells, houses, clocks, hills, graves, &c.*
井邊 'Tsing ,pien, *side of well.* 相連 ,Siang .lien, *connected.*
井水 'Tsing 'shui, *well water.* 天熱 ,T'ien jëh, *hot weather.*
天井 ,T'ien 'tsing, *square court.* 晚上 Wan' shang', *at evening.*
共井 Kung' 'tsing, *same well.* 掘開 Kiüëh ,k'ai, *dig open.*

鹹水 Hien 'shui, *salt water.* 弔桶 Tiau' 't'ung, *hanging*
   [*village.*   *bucket.*   [*rope.*
同鄉 T'ung, hiang, *same* 麻繩 Ma .sheng, *hempen*
宅子 Tseh 'tsï, *homestead.* 深淺 Shen 't'sien, *deep,*
                                              shallow.   [*ter.*
鄰舍 Lin she', *neighbours.* 挑水 T'iau 'shui, *carry wa-*
田地 T'ien ti', *cultivated land.* 打水 Ta 'shui, *take up water.*
弔水 Tiau' 'shui, *raise water.* 車水 C'he 'shui, *pump water.*
瓶放在井裏 .p'ing fang' tsai' 'tsing 'li, *place the bottle
   in the well.*
同鄉共井的人 .t'ung, hiang kung' 'tsing tih .jen, *men
   of the same village and a common well.*
晚上坐在井邊 wan' shang' tso' tsai' 'tsing ,pien, *at
   night they sat by the well.*
井水有些鹹 'tsing 'shui 'yeu ,sie .hien, *the water in the
   well is a little salt.*   [*bucket.*
弔桶放下去 tiau' 't'ung fang' hia' c'hü', *let down the*
打水的人 'ta 'shui tih .jen, *the water bearer.*
挑水回去 ,t'iau 'shui .hwei c'hü', *carry the water back.*
舀起水來 ,yau 'c'hi 'shui .lai, *take up water.*
牛車水 .nieu ,c'he 'shui, *the bullock pumped water.*
井掘開來 'tsing kiueh ,k'ai .lai, *the well was dug.*
用麻繩弔起桶來 yung' .ma .sheng tiau' 'c'hi 't'ung
   .lai, *draw up water with a rope.*
井的上邊有車 'tsing tih shang' ,pien 'yeu ,c'he, *above
   the well is a machine.*

LESSON 34. DINNER.

[*thern dialect.*
兒 .Rï, *terminal particle placed after most nouns in the nor-*
便飯 Pien' fan', *ordinary meal.* 再喝 Tsai' hoh, *drink again.*
不過 Puh kwo', *only* (initial). 賜飯 Tsï' fan', *grant me rice.*
罷了 Pa' 'liau, *only* (final). 廚房 .C'hu .fang, *kitchen.*
停 .T'ing, *wait.* 雞湯 ,Ki ,t'ang, *fowl broth.*
一會 Yih hwei', *a little; once.* 燕窩 Yen' ,wo, *birds' nest.*
擺飯 'Pai fan', *spread dinner.* 添 ,T'ien, *add; give more.*
上菜 Shang' t'sai', *put the* 飽了 'Pau 'liau, *satisfied.*
   dishes on the table. 倒茶 'Tau .c'ha, *pour out tea.*

LESSON 36. BUYING LAND.

地主 Ti' 'chu, *owner of land.* 相近 ,Siang kin', *near.*
步弓 Pu', kung, *measure of 5* 結實 Kièh shïh, *firm.*
恐怕 K'ung p'a', *lest.* [*feet.* 一畝 Yih 'meu, *one meu.*
街上, Kiai shang', *on the street.* 畝半 Meu pan', *meu & a half.*
鄉裏, Hiang 'li, *in the country.* 文約 .Wen yoh, *deed of sale.*
隣舍 .Lin she', *neighbours.* 中人 ,Chung .jen, *middleman.*
十吊 Shïh tiau', *ten strings.* 名兒 .Ming .rï, *name.*
大錢 Ta' .t'sien, *large cash.* 代筆 Tai' pih, *a writer.*
舊 Kieu', *old.* 打聽 'Ta ,t'ing, *to inquire.*
破 P'o', *broken.* 找尋 'Chau .siün, *to seek.*

我要買地 'wo yau' 'mai ti', *I wish to buy land.*
在大街上 tsai' ta' ,kiai shang', *in the great street.*
你替我打聽 'ni t'i' 'wo 'ta ,t'ing, *inquire for me.*
我找尋了一塊 'wo ,chau .siün 'liau yih k'wei', *I have found a piece.*
在大街南面 tsai' ta' ,kiai .nan mien', *on the south side of the great street.*
找一個中厚人 'chau yih ko' ,chung .heu' .jen, *find me an honest man.*
請他做代筆 't'sing ,t'a tso' tai' pih, *invite him to be the writer.*
代筆的人寫的文約 tai' pih tih .jen 'sie tih .wen yoh, *the writer will write the deed of sale.*
你做中人可以 'ni tso' ,chung .jen 'k'o 'i, *you can be the middle man.*
兩下說說明白 'liang hia' shwoh shwoh .ming peh, *speak clearly on both sides.*
買地的主人 mai' ti' tih 'chu .jen, *the proprietor who sells the land.* [*not?*
有錢沒有錢 'yeu .t'sien muh 'yeu .t'sien, *has he money or*
有舊房子 'yeu kieu' .fang 'tsï, *there is an old house.*
還在地上 .hwan tsai' ti' shang', *still on the ground.*
這個總要折了 che' ko' 'tsung yau' t'seh 'liau, *this must be pulled down.* [*land.*
地有四畝半 ti' 'yeu sï' 'meu pan', *there are 4½ mow of*

二十兩銀子一畝 rĭ' shĭh 'liang .yin 'tsï yih 'meu, *twenty taels a mow.*

還有一塊地在鄉裏 .hwan 'yeu yih k'wei' ti' tsai' ,hiang 'li, *there is a piece of land in the country.*

鄉舍人家好的 .hiang she' ,jen ,kia 'hau tih, *the neighbours are good.*

十吊大錢 shĭh tiau' ta' .t'sien, *ten strings of large cash.*

把步弓量量看 'pa pu' ,kung liang' liang' k'an', *measure it with the rod.*

二百五十步一畝 rĭ' peh 'wu shĭh pu' yih 'meu, *250 pu make a mow.*   [*also called a kung.*

一步也教一弓 yih pu' 'ye kiau' yih ,kung, *a pu is*

五尺一步 'wu c'hĭh yih pu', *five feet make one pu.*

這麼小恐怕不彀 che' 'mo 'siau 'k'ung-p'a' puh keu', *this is small, and I fear it will not be enough.*

LESSON 37. TIGERS.

老虎 'Lau 'hu, *tiger.* 不理 Puh 'li, *not to care for.*
許 Hü, *to promise.* 菜園 T'sai' ,yuen, *veg. garden.*
賞 'Shang, *reward.* [thers. 啣 .Hien, *to take in the mouth.*
虎豹 'Hu pau', *tigers and panthers.* 偷竊 T'eu' t'sih, *to steal.*
擺設 Pai' shèh, *to set out.* 凶 ,Hiung, *violent.*
陷坑 .Hien ,k'eng, *a pitfall.* 害處 Hai' c'hu', *injuries.*
地弩 Ti' 'nu, *a spring arrow.* 野獸 'Ye sheu', *wild animals.*
擒 .K'in, *to catch.* 竹林 Chuh .lin, *bamboo grove.*
引誘 'Yin 'yeu, *to tempt.* 後面 Heu' mien', *behind.*

鎮安老虎多 ,Chen ,ngan 'lau 'hu ,to, *at the city of Chen-n gan tigers are numerous.*

害城裏百姓 hai' .c'heng 'li peh sing' *they injure the people in the city.*

有人能殺老虎的 'yeu jen .neng shah 'lau 'hu tih, *there are persons who can kill tigers.*

我許了他們 'wo 'hü 'liau ,t'a .men, *I promised them.*

殺一虎賞五十千 shah yih 'hu 'shang 'wu shĭh ,t'sien, *if they killed a tiger they should receive fifty thousand reward.*   [*placed.*

住的人擺設 chu' tih .jen (pai' shèh) *the inhabitants*

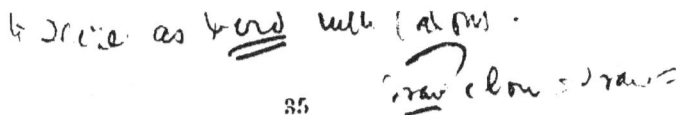

陷坑和地弩 .hien ,k'eng .ho ti' ,nu. *pitfalls and spring bows.*

不能擒得他 puh .neng k'in teh ,t'a. *they could not catch them.*

用山羊引誘他 yung' ,shan ,yang 'yin 'yeu ,t'a, *they used goats to entice them.*

老虎不理 'lau 'hu puh 'li, *the tigers took no notice.*

房屋後面有菜園 fang uh heu' mien' 'yeu t'sai' yuen, *behind the houses are vegetable gardens.*

夜裏有人走到園中 ye' 'li 'yeu ,jen 'tseu tau' .yuen ,chung, *if at night a man walks into the garden.*

老虎已經啣了他去 'lau 'hu 'i ,king .hien 'liau ,t'a k'ü', *a tiger has already taken him away in his mouth.*

夜裏沒有偷竊東西的 ye' 'li muh 'yeu t'eu' t'sih ,tung ,si tih, *at night there is no one to steal.*

怕老虎不敢來 p'a' 'lau 'hu puh 'kan .lai, *fearing tigers they dare not come.*

LESSON 38. ELEPHANTS.

野象 'Ye siang', *wild elephant.*
白象 Peh siang', *white do.*
法子 Fah 'tsï, *method.*
供役 Kung' yih, *service.*
掘 Kiueh, *to dig.*
鋪席 ,P'u sih, *spread mats.*
蓋好 Kai' 'hau, *cover over.*
打鑼 'Ta .lo, *beat gongs.*
趕 ,Kan, *drive.*
打鼓 'Ta 'ku, *beat drums.*

放礮 Fang' p'au', *fire guns.*
餓 Wo', *hungry; to starve.*
點頭 'Tien .t'eu, *to nod the head.*
斜 .Sie, *inclined; crooked.*
撒 C'heh, *to push away.*
終身 ,Chung ,shen, *whole life.*
馱 .T'o, *carry on back.*
服事 Fuh sï', *to serve.*
餧 Wei', *to feed.*

西南有野象 ,si .nan 'yeu 'ye' siang', *in the south west there are wild elephants.*

本地人用法子 'pen ti' .jen yung' fah 'tsï, *the natives use methods.*

誘他們做供役的 'yeu ,t'a .men tso' kung' yih tih, *to tempt them to become serviceable.*

掘地坑鋪席子蓋好 kiueh ti' ,k'eng ,p'u sih 'tsï kai' 'hau, *they dig a pit and cover it well with mats.*

再加泥土在上 tsai‘ ,kia .ni ’t‘u tsai‘ shang‘, *they also place earth upon the mats.*
好像平地似的 ’hau siang‘ .p‘ing ti‘ sï‘ tih, *so that it is like the level ground.*
好幾百個人 ’hau ’ki peh ko‘ .jen, *several hundred men.*
打鑼打鼓放礮 ’ta .lo ’ta ’ku fang‘ p‘au‘, *beat gongs and drums, and fire guns.*
趕象走過陷他下去 ,kan siang‘ ’tseu kwo‘ .hien ,t‘a hia‘ c‘hü‘, *they drive the elephant past and they fall in.*
身體重坑深 ,shen ’t‘i chung‘ ,k‘eng ,shen, *he is heavy in body, and the pit is deep.*
不能出來 puh .neng c‘huh .lai, *he cannot come out.*
就餓他幾天 tsieu‘ wo‘ ,t‘a ’ki ,t‘ien, *they then keep him without food for several days.*
後來問他 heu‘ .lai wen‘ ,t‘a, *afterwards they ask him.*
做供役肯不肯 tso‘ kung‘ yuh ’k‘eng puh ’k‘eng, *if he is willing or not to do service.*
象點了頭 siang‘ ,tien ’liau .t‘eu, *the elephant nods his head.*
地坑面前撒去土 ti‘ ,k‘eng mien‘ .t‘sien c‘hêh c‘hü‘ ’t‘u, *in front of the pit they remove the earth.*
開一條斜路 ,k‘ai yih .t‘iau .sie lu‘, *open an inclined path.*
給象好走上 kih siang‘ ’hau ’tseu shang‘, *so that the elephant can walk out.*
一點了頭 yih ’tien ’liau .t‘eu, *if he once nods his head.*
終身要服事人 ,chung ,shen yau‘ fuh sï‘ .jen, *he will serve man all his life.*
至死不變 chï‘ ’sï puh pien‘, *till death never changing.*
性情㝍信實 sing‘ .t‘sing tsui‘ sin‘ shïh, *his disposition is very faithful.* [carry.
一個象能馱 yih ko‘ siang‘ .neng .t‘o, *once elephant can*
千斤礮一位 ,t‘sien ,king p‘au‘ yih wei‘, *a cannon weighing a thousand pounds.* [nod his head.
象不點頭 siang‘ puh ’tien .t‘eu, *if the elephant does not*
不教他出來 puh kiau‘ ,t‘a c‘huh .lai, *they do not let him come out.*

兩三回問他 'liang ,san .hwei wen‘ ,t‘a, *they ask him two or three times.* [*death.*
餓死也有的 wo‘ 'sï ’ye 'yeu tih, *some are starved to*
總不點頭 ’tsung puh ’tien .t‘eu, *any how they will not nod their head.*

LESSON 39. SILVER MINES.

載來 Tsai‘ .lai, *to bring.* 內地 Nui‘ ti‘, *China proper.*
銀礦 .Yin ’k‘wang, *silver-ore* 漢朝 Han‘ .c‘hau, *Han dynasty.*
mine.
收稅 ,Sheu ’shui, *receive cus-* 特意 T‘eh i‘, *purposely.*
利息 Li‘ sih, *profit.* [*toms.* 兵丁 ,Ping ,ting, *soldiers.*
邊外 ,Pien wai‘, *beyond the* 交鋒 ,Kiau ,fung, *join battle.*
散 San‘, *to separate.* [*border.* 遣 ,C‘hien, *to send.* [*tle.*
關口 ,Kwan ’k‘eu, *border* 緬甸 ’Mien tien‘, *Birmah.*
custom house.   安南 ,Ngan .nan, *Cochin-china.*
上山 Shang‘ ,shan, *go up a hill.* 廠丁 ’C‘hang ,ting, *office ser-*
廠 ’C‘hang, *large house or office.*   vants.
幾十 ’Ki shïh, *several tens.* 老早 ’Lau ’tsau, *long since.*
中國出銀子呢 ,Chung kweh c‘huh .yin ’tsï .ni, *does China produce silver?* [*had silver.*
本來有銀子的 ’pen .lai ’yeu .yin ’tsï tih, *originally it*
如今內地沒有的 .ju ,kin nui‘ ti‘ muh ’yeu tih, *now there is none in this country.* [*that have silver.*
有銀礦的地方 ’yeu .yin ’k‘wang tih ti‘ .fang, *places*
老早都取盡了 ’lau ’tsau ,tu ’t‘sü ,tsin‘ ’liau, *it has long since been taken all away.*
緬甸載來有的 ’Mien tien‘ tsai‘ .lai ’yeu tih, *some is brought from Birmah.*
安南銀子也有 ’Ngan .nan .yin ’tsï ’ye ’yeu, *in Cochin-china there is also silver.* [*Han dynasty.*
漢朝的時候 Han‘ .c‘hau tih .shï heu‘, *in the time of the*
安南也在中國裏面 ,Ngan .nan ’ye tsai‘ ,Chung kweh ’li mien‘, *Cochin-china also was a part of China.*
緬甸有大山廠 ’Mien tien‘ ’yeu ’Ta ,shan ’c‘hang, *in Birmah there is the Ta-shan silver-mine* [*of Yün-nan.*
在雲南邊外 tsai‘ .Yün .nan ,pien wai‘, *outside the border*

安南有宋星厰 Ngan ,nan 'yeu Sung‛ ,sing 'c‛hang, in Cochin-china is the Sung sing silver-mine.

在廣西邊外 tsai‛ 'Kwang ,si ,pien wai‛, beyond the border of Kwang-si.

從前本國與緬甸打仗 .t‛sung .t‛sien 'pen kweh .ü 'Mien tien‛ ,ta chang‛, formerly our country went to war with Birmah.

兩面兵馬交鋒 'liang mien‛ ,ping 'ma ,kiau ,fung, the two armies of soldiers and horses met in battle.

厰丁已經散了 'c‛hang ,ting 'i ,king san‛ 'liau, the miners were all scattered.

沒有人去要銀子 muh 'yeu ,jen c‛hü‛ yau‛ ,yin 'tsï, no one went to seek silver.

後來設立官府收稅 heu‛ .lai shèh lih ,kwan fu‛ ,sheu shui‛, afterwards they appointed officers to collect duties.

特意管這個事 t‛eh i‛ 'kwan che‛ ko‛ shï‛, they attend specially to this matter.

上山去探礦裏的銀子 shang‛ ,shan c‛hü‛ t‛sai 'k‛wang 'li tih .yin 'tsï, they went up the hill to seek for the mines.

必定先要過關口完稅 pih ting‛ ,sien yau‛ kwo‛ ,kwan 'k‛eu .wen shui‛, they must first pass the custom-house and pay the duty.

LESSON 40. WATER.

吃慣 C‛hih ,kwan, eat habi-[tually.
差慣 ,C‛hai ,kwan, send ha-
老夫 'Lau ,fu, I. [bitually.
宿 Suh, to pass the night.
洗臉 'Si 'lien, wash the face.
盂 .Ü, small bowl.
澄清 .C‛heng ,t‛sing, to cleanse.
顏色 .Yen seh, colour.
氣味 C‛hi‛ wei‛, taste.
大概 Ta‛ kai‛, the most.
無價之寶 .wu kia‛ ,chï 'pau, an inestimable treasure.

獨是 Tuh shï‛, only.
常久 .C‛hang 'kieu, long time.
兩樣 'Liang yang‛, different.
朋友 .P‛eng yeu‛, friends.
澆灌 ,Kiau kwan‛, to water.
乾枯 ,Kan ,k‛u, withered.
鹼 ,Kien, soda.
鹼氣 ,Kien c‛hi‛, soda vapour.
土氣 'T‛u c‛hi‛, exhalations.
晒 Shai‛, to dry in the sun.

五穀百菓 'wu kuh peh 'kwo, *the five kinds of grain and the hundred fruits.*

甘肅地方水最少寶在無價之寶, Kan suh ti' ,fang 'shui 'sui 'shau, shih tsai' .wu kia', chī 'pau, *water in Kan-suh is very scarce and is indeed of priceless value.*

老夫差慣一個用人到蘭州 'lau ,fu ,c'hai ,kwan yih ko' yung' ,jen tau' .Lan ,cheu, *I used to send messenger regularly to Lan-cheu.* [*he slept at a lodging house.*]

夜裏宿在客店 ye' ,li suh tsai' k'eh tien', *in the night*

有一盂水送客洗臉 yeu yih ,ü 'shui sung' k'eh 'si 'lien, *a small bason of water was given to the lodgers to wash their faces.*

洗好了臉不可以丟了水 'si 'hau 'liau 'lien puh 'k'o 'i ,tieu 'liau 'shui, *after washing their faces the water must not be throw away.*

店家把水澄清了再用 tien' ,kia 'pa 'shui .c'heng ,t'sing 'liau tsai' yung', *the landlord cleansed the water to be used again.*

水不通流的就叫死水 'shui puh ,t'ung .lieu tih tsieu' kiau' 'sī 'shui, *water that does not flow is called dead water.*

時候常久顏色要變 .shī heu' ,c'hang 'kieu .yen-seh yau' pien', *after a long time the colour changes.*

氣味也不好不可以吃 c'hi'-wei' 'ye puh 'hau puh 'k'o 'i c'hih, *it smells bad and is not good to drink.*

大概地方這樣的 ta'kai' ti' .fang che' yang' tih, *in most places it is so.* [yang' tih, *only in Kan-suh it is different.*

獨是甘肅不是這樣的 tuh shī', Kan suh puh shī' che'

已經常久水得了土氣就清好吃得 'i ,king' .c'hang 'kieu 'shui teh 'liau t'ü c'hi' tsieu' ,t'sing 'hau c'hih teh, *after a long time the water, through the influence of the soil becomes clear and may be drunk.*

我有朋友在寧夏做官 'wo 'yeu .p'eng yeu' tsai' .Ning-hia' tso' ,kwan, *I have a friend who was a magistrate at Ning-hia.*

他告訴我 ,t'a kau' su' 'wo, *he informed me.*

甘肅省處處能下雨幾好, Kan suh 'seng c'hu' c'hu'

.neng hia' 'ü ,t'sai ,hau, *everywhere if Kan-suh province if rain falls it is well.*

不過寧夏兩樣的 puh kwo' .Ning hia' 'liang yang' ,tih, *only at Ning-hia it is different.*

不但不要下雨 puh tan' puh yau' hia' 'ü, *not only do they not desire it to rain.* [*that it should rain.*]

而且怕要下雨 rï t'sie p'a' yau' hia' 'ü, *they even fear*

因為這個地多鹼氣 ,yin .wei che' ko' ti' ,to ,kien c'hi', *because here there is much soda in the soil.*

雨太多日頭曬了就有鹼氣上升 'ü t'ai' ,to jïh .t'eu shai' 'liau tsieu' 'yeu ,kien c'hi' shang' ,sheng, *if there is much rain, then when the sun shines the vapour of the soda ascends.*

相近看着像雪一樣花草都要乾枯 ,siang kin' ,k'an' choh ,siang siuèh yih yang' , ,hwa 't'sau ,tu yau' ,kan ,k'u, *seen near it looks like snow, and the flowers and grass wither.*

所以一年不下雨也不在心上 so 'i yih .nien puh hia' 'ü 'ye puh tsai' ,sin shang', *therefore if for a year it does not rain, it matters little.*

寧夏稻田米最多 .Ning hia' tau' .tien 'mi tsui' ,to, *at Ning-hia rice is grown in the fields in great quantity.*

單靠黃河水澆灌 ,tan k'au' .Hwang .ho 'shui ,kiau kwan', *it relies on the Yellow river alone for watering.*

水渾倒底肥的狠 'shui ,hwen 'tau ,ti .fei tih 'hen, *the water is muddy but very fertilizing.*

水到的落地五穀百菓都是發旺的 'shui tau' tih loh ti' 'wu kuh peh 'kwo ,tu shï' fah wang' tih, *in the parts reached by the water, the grain and fruits are abundant.*

不必澆糞在上 puh pih' ,kiau fen' tsai' shang', *it does not need to be manured.*

田裏的水稍微清一點就放他回去 .tien 'li tih 'shui ,shau .wei ,t'sing yih 'tien tsieu' fang' ,t'a .hwei c'hü', *when the water in the fields has become clearer it is allowed to return.*

LESSON 41. COALS AT PEKING.

建都 Kien' ,tu, *establish a capital.* 竈頭 Tsau' .t'eu, *cooking range.*

城池 .C‘heng .c‘hï, *wall & moat.* 炊 ,C‘hui, *to burn.*
朝廷 .C‘hau .t‘ing, *the court.* 煮 'Chu, *to boil.* [*pieces.*
水路 'Shui lu‘, *canals & rivers.* 敲碎 ,C‘hiau sui‘, *break in*
旱路 Han‘ lu‘, *roads.* 灰印 ,Hwei yin‘, *chalk mark.*
柴薪 .C‘hai, sin, *wood for fuel.* 半文 Pan‘ .wen, *half a cash.*
一項 Yih hiang‘, *one kind.* 計重 Ki‘ chung‘, *the amount.*
不足 Puh tsuh, *not enough.* 分兩 Fen‘ 'liang, *weight.* [*cit.*
有餘 Yeu .ü, *superabundance.* 補足 'Pu tsuh, *make up a defi-*

中國建都在北京一千多年以前, Chung kweh kien‘ ,tu tsai‘ Peh ,king yih ,t‘sien, to .nien 'i .t‘sien, *China had its capital at Peking more than a thousand years ago.*

頭一次在遼朝的時候 .t‘eu yih t‘sï‘ tsai‘ .Liau .c‘hau tih .shï heu‘, *first in the time of the Liau dynasty.*

京都的城池宮殿朝廷廟宇花苑都是完全 ,king ,tu tih .c‘heng .c‘hï ,kung tien‘ .c‘hau .t‘ing miau‘ 'ü ,hwa .yuen ,tu shï‘ .wan .t‘siuen, *in the capital, the walls and moat, halls, palace, temples and gardens, are all complete.*

水路旱路歷代下來有了 'shui lu‘ han‘ lu‘ lih tai‘ hia‘ .lai 'yeu 'liau, *there have been canals and roads through successive generations till now.*

也有如同天生成攻的好處 'ye 'yeu .ju .t‘ung ,t‘ien ,sheng .c‘heng ;kung tih 'hau c‘hü‘, *there are also natural advantages seeming like the gift of heaven.*

比方柴薪一項東西 'pi ,fang .c‘hai ,sin yih hiang‘ ,tung ,si, *for example, there is for one thing a supply of wood for fuel.*

西山的出產有好煤 ,si ,shan tih c‘huh 'c‘han 'yeu 'hau .mei, *among the productions of the western mountains there is good coals.*

好做燒火的供用 'hau tso‘ ,shau 'ho tih kung‘ yung‘, *it is serviceable for burning.*

父老的話相傳下來 fu‘ 'lau tih hwa‘ ,siang .c‘hwen hia‘ .lai, *in the words of old men coming down by tradition.*

燒不盡的西山煤 ,shau puh tsin‘ tih ,si ,shan .mei, *the coal of the western mountains cannot be burned out.*

但是京裏的人一天多一天 tan‘ shï‘ ,king 'li tih

,jen yih ,t'icu ,to yih ,t'ien, *but the inhabitants of the capital grow daily more numerous.*

竈頭上炊煮用的火一天多一天 tsau' .t'eu, shang' ,c'hui 'chu yung' tih 'ho yih ,t'ien ,to yih ,t'ien, *the burning and cooking in the kitchens increases daily.*

煤價一日貴一日 .mei kia' yih ji̇̆h kwei' yih ji̇̆h, *the price of coal is daily higher.*

煤敲碎了每塊上打一灰印賣錢三文計重二斤十二兩 .mei ,c'hiau sui' 'liau 'mei k'wei' shang' ta' yih ,hwei yin' mai' .t'sien ,san .wen ki' chung' rï' ,kin shi̇̆h .rï 'liang, *the coal was broken in pieces, on each piece a chalk mark was made; it was sold for three cash, and weighed two catties and twelve ounces.*

現在價錢一樣一塊的分兩不過一斤多點 hien' tsai' kia' .t'sien yih yang' yih k'wei' tih fen' 'liang puh kwo' yih ,kin ,to 'tien, *at present the price is the same, but the weight of one piece is not much more than a catty.*

直隸省獲鹿縣有煤廠 Chi̇̆h li' 'sheng Hwoh luh hien' 'yeu .mei 'c'hang, *in the province of Chi̇̆h-le, there is a coal-mine at the district of Hwoh-luh.*

離京不過六百里 .li ,king puh kwo' luh peh 'li, *it is distant from the capital only two hundred miles.*

西山不足獲鹿的有餘可以補足 ,si ,shan puh tsuh Hwoh luh tih 'yeu .ü 'k'o 'i 'pu tsuh, *the western mountains if deficient can be supplemented from the additional supply at Hwoh-luh.*

LESSON 42. JUNK NAVIGATION.

停不得 .T'ing puh teh, *you must not stop.*
走不過 'Tseu puh kwo', *you cannot pass.*
新開河 ,Sin ,k'ai .ho, *newly opened canal.*
但不過 Tan' puh kwo', *only.*
老口子 'Lau 'k'eu 'tsï, *old mouth river.*
避開來 Pi' ,k'ai .lai, *to pass by and avoid.*
復寶沙 Fuh 'pau ,sha, *name of a sand bank.* [chor-
木錨 Muh .mau, *wooden anchor.* 鐵錨 T'ieh .mau, *iron an-*

羅盤 .Lo .p'an, *mariner's compass.* 稍爲 'Sau .wei, *a little.*

海船從上海黃浦口岸開去 'hai .c'hwen .t'sung Shang' 'hai .Hwang p'u' 'k'eu ngau' ,k'ai c'hü', *a sea junk sets sail from the banks of the Hwang-pu at Shanghai.*

向東行五十里出吳淞口入洋 hiang', tung .hing 'wu shïh 'li c'huh .Wu ,sung 'k'eu juh .yang, *going eastward it travels for fifty li passing out of the Wu-sung river mouth.*

環繞復寶沙走到崇明的新開河 .hwan'jau fuh 'pau ,sha 'tseu tau' .T'sung .ming tih ,Sin ,k'ai .ho, *winding round the Fuh-pau bank, it sails to Sin-k'ai-ho in T'sung-ming.*

共計一百一十里 kung' ki' yih peh yih shïh 'li, *it numbers in all one hundred and ten li.*

又七十里到十激就是內洋 yeu' t'sih shïh 'li tau' Shïh hiau' tsieu' shï' nui' .yang, *there are seventy more li to Shïh-hiau, which is in the inner ocean.*

這裏可以停船 che' 'li 'k'o 'i .t'ing .c'hwen, *here you can stop the junk.*

此地也好等候順風放洋 't'sï ti' 'ye 'hau 'teng heu' shun' ,feng fang' .yang, *here also you will do well to wait for a fair wind to go to sea.*

又向東走到舍山 yeu' hiang' ,tung 'tseu tau' .She ,shan, *again going eastward you proceed to She-shan island.*

這山上沒有百姓住的 che' ,shan shang' muh 'yeu peh sing' chu' tih, *on this island there are no persons residing.*

船停不得不能下錨 .c'hwen .t'ing puh teh puh .neng hia' .mau, *the vessel cannot stop here, it is impossible to cast anchor.*

這兒向東出大洋往北稍爲偏東 che' .rï hiang' ,tung c'huh ta' .yang 'wang pei (peh) 'sau .wei ,p'ien ,tung, *from this spot going eastward vessels go out to sea and proceed north and a little to the eastward.*

到黃河老口子稍爲向南有五條沙埂 tau' .Hwang .ho 'lau 'k'eu 'tsï 'sau .wei hiang' .nan 'yeu 'wu .t'iau ,sha 'keng, *a little to the south of the old mouth of the Yellow river there are five sand banks.*

遇着東風總要想慮淺擱 ü' choh ,tung ,feng 'tsung

yau' 'siang lü' 't'sien koh, *should you meet with an east wind, you must be looking out against shallows and grounding.*

該當避開來 kai, tang pi', k'ai .lai, *you should avoid them.*

統歸江南地界 't'ung ,kwei ,kiang .nan ti' kiai', *it all belongs to the territory of Kiang-nan.*

用羅盤定見方向 yung' .lu .p'an ting' kien' ,fang hiang', *use the compass to fix your course.*

換方向偏東一個字 hwan' ,fang hiang' ,p'ien ,tung yih ko' tsï, *change your course and go one point more to the eastward.*

爛泥用木錨硬泥用鐵錨 .lan .ni yung' muh .mau, ying' .ni yung' t'ieh .mau, *with a soft bottom use the wooden anchor, and with a hard bottom the iron one.*

LESSON 43. FURS.

運來的 Yün' .lai tih, *imported.*
北口外 Peh 'k'eu wai', *beyond the north boundary.*
貂 ,Tiau, *sable.*　狐狸 .Hu ,li, *fox.*
裏子 'Li 'tsï, *lining.*　面子 Mien' 'tsï, *facing.*
趁 C'heng', *take advantage of.* 弔毛 Tiau' .mau, *let fall hair.*
不大不小 Puh ta' puh siau', *neither great nor little, aver-*
灰鼠 ,Hwei 'shu, *grey squirrel.* 狼 .Lang, *wolf.*　　[age.
潮 .C'hau, *damp.*　　褥 Juh, *rug.*
坑 K'ang', *brick couch.*　晾 Liang, *to air.*

貂皮從那裏運來的 ,tiau .p'i .t'sung 'na 'li yün' .lai tih, *whence are sables imported?*

北口外蒙古地方來的 peh 'k'eu wai' .Meng 'ku ti' ,fang .lai tih, *they come from beyond the northern barrier, from the land of the Mongols.*

這個袍子是狐嗉皮做的 che' ko' .p'au 'tsï shï .hu su' .p'i tso' tih, *this long coat is made of the fur from foxes' necks.*

八十個灰鼠皮做的 pah shïh ko' ,hwei 'shu .p'i tso' tih, *made of eighty squirrels skins.*

皮裏的靴頭一雙 .p'i 'li tih ,hiue .t'eu yih ,shwang, *a pair of skin lined half boots.*

狼皮好做馬褂 .lang .p'i 'hau tso' 'ma kwa', *wolf skin can be made into jackets.*

價錢頂貴是貂皮 chia' .t'sien 'ting kwei' shï' ,tiau .p'i, *the highest in price is sable.*

貂皮套子價錢不大不小肆拾兩 ,tiau.p'i tau' 'tsï chia' .t'sien puh ta' puh 'siau sï' shïh liang', *a sable coat costs more or less forty taels.*

這個皮好不弔毛 che' ko' .p'i 'hau puh ,tiau .mau, *this fur is good, the hair will not fall off.*

做過衣裳的皮不買 tso' kwo' ,i .shang tih .p'i puh 'mai, *skins that have been made into clothes I do not buy.*

下雨天皮衣服受潮要弔毛 hia' 'ü ,t'ien .p'i ,i fuh sheu' .c'hau yau' tiau' .mau, *in time of rain fur clothes become damp and the hair will fall off.*

趁這好天氣將皮衣服晾晾收了 c'heng' che' 'hau ,t'ien c'hi' ,tsiang .p'i ,i fuh liang' liang' ,sheu 'liau, *taking advantage of this good weather give your fur clothes an airing and put them away.*

坑上鋪着羊皮褥 k'ang' shang' ,p'u choh .yang .p'i juh, *upon the brick couch was spread a goat-skin rug.*

地下生着炭火爐 ti' hia' ,sheng choh t'an' 'ho lu', *below he had lighted a charcoal fire.*

LESSON 44. IMPORTED FOREIGN MANUFACTURES.

羽毛 .Ü .mau, *camlets.* 斜文 ,Sie .wen, *striped.*
嗶嘰 Pih 'chi, *long ells.* 本色 'Pen seh, *unbleached.*
花洋布 ,Hwa .yang pu', *chintz; printed cottons.*
本色洋布 'Pen seh .yang pu', *grey shirtings.*
漂白洋布 ,P'iau peh .yang pu', *white shirtings.*
桂花布 ,Kwei ,hwa pu', *spotted stuffs.*
斜文布 .Sie .wen pu', *American drills.*
花旗布 ,Hwa .c'hi pu', *domestics.*
漂白 ,P'iau peh, *bleached.*
天青 ,T'ien ,t'sing, *purple.* 單子 ,Tan 'tsï, *a statement.*
羽毛每一疋十五兩 .ü .mau 'mei yih p'ih shïh 'wu 'liang, *one piece of camlet costs fifteen taels.* [*purple long ells.*
天青嗶嘰馬褂 ,t'ien ,t'sing pih 'chi ,ma kwa', *a jacket of*
花洋布好買不好買 ,hwa .yang pu' 'hau 'mai puh 'hau 'mai, *can printed cottons be bought or not?*

本色洋布漂白洋布全沒有人要'pen seh .yang pu' ,p'iau peh .yang pu' .t'siuen muh 'yeu .jen yau', *both for grey shirtings and white there is no demand.*

棧房裏花旗布裝的多 chan' .fang 'li ,hwa .c'hi pu' ,chwang tih ,to, *in the warehouse there are stowed domestics in large quantities.* [*there is also no small quantity.*

斜紋布也不少有 .sie .wen pu' 'ye puh 'shau, *of drills*

有客商要花洋布 'yeu k'eh ,shang yau' ,hwa .yang pu', *there are dealers who want printed cottons.*

漂白的桂花洋布沒有顏色的就有 ,p'iau peh tih ,kwei ,hwa .yang pu' muh 'yeu 'yen seh tih tsieu' 'yeu, *there are no white spotted cotton cloths, but there are coloured ones.*

洋布比從先賤 .yang pu' 'pi .t'sung ,sien tsien', *foreign cottons are cheaper than before.*

此刻不太平客商不敢買 't'sï k'eh puh t'ai' .p'ing k'eh ,shang puh 'kan 'mai, *at present times are not peaceful, and dealers dare not buy.*

洋布受了海潮有毛病的 .yang pu' sheu' 'liau 'hai .c'hau 'yeu .mau .p'ing tih, *cottons that imbibed sea damp are damaged.*

洋布較從前價值稍輕 .yang pu' kiau' .t'sung .t'sien kia' chïh 'sau ,k'ing, *cotton goods compared with what they formerly were are a little cheaper.*

今後的東西甚樣價錢開單子 ,kin heu' tih ,tung ,si shen' yang' kia' .t'sien ,k'ai ,tan 'tsï, *from this time the prices of articles will be stated in a tabular form.*

LESSON. 45. FOREIGN TRIBUTE.

年紀 .Nien 'ki, *'years; time.*
進貢 Tsin' kung', *present tribute.*
褲子 K'u' 'tsï, *trowsers.* [bute.
靠 K'au', *to rely on; lean.*
靠西 K'au' ,si, *lying in the west.*
盔 K'wei, *helmet.*
甲 Chiah, *coat of mail.* [tal.
水晶 'Shui ,tsing, *rock-crys-*

出名 C'huh .ming, *to obtain* [*fame.*
宰相 'Tsae siang', *chief minis-*
犀牛 Si .nieu, *rhinoceros.* [ter.
駱駝 Loh .t'o, *camel.*
塗金 .T'u ,kin, *gild a surface.*
描金 .Miau ,kin, *gild figures.*
灑金 'Sa ,kin, *gild in spots.*
綿 .Mien, *soft; cotton.*

湯王的年紀有出名的宰相名叫伊尹 ,T'ang
.wang tih .nien 'ki 'yeu c'huh .ming tih 'tsae siang' .ming
kiau' ,I 'yin, *in the time of T'ang-wang there was a celebrated minister of state called I-yin.*

定見各國進貢的規矩 ting' kien' koh kweh tsin'
,kung tih ,kwei chü', *he fixed the regulations for the presents brought from various countries.*

東面有魚皮的褲子和快劍 ,tung mien' 'yeu .ü
.p'i tih k'u' 'tsï .ho k'wai' kien', *from the east were brought
fish-skin trowsers and sharp swords.*

南邊貢珠子象牙犀牛角 .nan ,pien kung' ,chu
'tsï, siang' .ya ,si .nieu kioh, *from the south were brought
pearls, elephant's tusks, and rhinoceros horn.*

靠西面的進貢用紅綠顏色牛毛旗子龍角
和大龜子 k'au' ,si mien' tih tsin' kung' yung' .hung
lüh .yen seh, .nieu .mau .c'hi 'tsï, .lung kioh .ho ta' ,kwei
'tsï, *those on the west brought a tribute, red and green dies,
buffalo-hair streamers, dragon horns, and large tortoises.*

北邊國都貢的駱駝和白馬 peh ,pien kweh tu',
kung' tih loh .t'o .ho peh 'ma, *the northern nations presented, camels and horses.*

明朝日本國進貢盔甲腰刀塗金的屏風灑
金手箱描金筆匣水晶數珠 .Ming .c'hau Jih
'pen kweh tsin' kung' ,k'wei chiah, yau' ,tau, .t'u ,chin tih
.p'ing ,feng, 'sa ,chin 'sheu ,siang, .miau ,chin pih hiah,
'shui ,tsing su' ,chu, *in the Ming dynasty, Japan sent as
tribute, helmets and coats of mail, belt knives, gilt embos-
sed screens, hand boxes spotted with gilt, pencil boxes
painted with gold, and crystal beads for numbering prayers.*

朝鮮出白綿紬出白綿紙 .C'hau ,sien c'huh peh
.mien .c'heu, c'huh peh .mien 'chï, *Corea produces soft
white silk, and soft white paper.*

馬三年進貢五十匹 'ma ,san .nien tsin' kung' 'wu
shih p'ih, *of horses there are fifty presented in three years.*

LESSON 46. THE EMPEROR'S SEAL.

以前 'I .t'sien, *before.* 方寸 ,Fang t'sun', *square inch.*

以後 'I hou', *after*.
璽 'Si, *government seal*.
印 Yin', *mandarin's seal*.
圖書 .T'u ,shu, *common seal*.
封 ,Feng, *confer royal title*.
橫 .Heng, *horizontal*.

天子 ,T'ien 'tsï, *son of heaven*.
尋常 .Siün .c'hang, *common*.
稱 ,C'heng, *to name*. [*acter*.
篆文 Chwen' .wen, *seal char-*
碰見 P'eng' chien'; *to meet*.
豎 Shu', *upright*.

秦朝以前百姓都可以身邊帶璽用金子銀子和玉做的 .T'sin .c'hau 'i .t'sien peh sing' ,tu 'k'o 'i ,shen ,pien tai' 'si yung', chin 'tsï .yin 'tsï .ho yüh tso' tih, *before the T'sin dynasty the people could wear a seal at their side, made of gold, silver and jade*.

大小不過方寸 ta' siau' puh kwo' ,fang t'sun', *they are in size only an inch square*.

朝代用大的也有 .c'hau-tai' yung' ta' tih 'ye 'you, *there are also dynasties that have used large ones*.

秦始皇以來天子一個人稱璽 T'sin 'shï .hwang 'i .lai ,t'ien 'tsï yih ko' .jen ,c'heng 'si, *from the time of Tsin-shï-hwang till now the word si is applied only to the seal of the son of heaven*.

官府所用的叫印尋常人所用的叫圖書 ,kwan 'fu 'so yung' tih kiau' yin', .siün .c'hang .jen 'so yung' tih kiau' .t'u ,shu, *those used by mandarins are called yin, official seals, and those of the common people t'u shu, common seals*.

皇帝的行璽封國都用的 .hwang ti' tih .hing 'si ,feng kweh ,tu yung' tih, *that called "emperor's travelling seal" is employed in conferring royal titles*.

皇帝的信璽是發兵用的 .hwang ti' tih sin' 'si shï' fah ,ping yung' tih, *"the faithful seal" is used in dispatching an army*.

不是皇帝不許用玉做圖書 puh shï' .hwang ti' puh 'hü yung' yüh tso' .t'u ,shu, *except the emperor no one is allowed to use a seal of jade*.

上面有刻的字受天之命皇帝壽昌 shang' mien' 'yeu k'eh tih tsï' sheu' ,t'ien ,chï ming' .hwang ti' sheu' ,c'hang, *upon it are engraven the words, receiving the decree of heaven, the emperor enjoys old age and prosperity*.

各朝刻的文各樣全是篆文 Koh .c'hau k'eh tih .wen koh yang' .t'siuen shï ch'wen' .wen, *each dynasty uses its peculiar inscription, all are in the seal character.*

天啟四年的時候在漳河北岸上 T'ien c'hi' sï' .nien tih .shï heu' tsai' ,Chwang-ho peh-ngan' shang', *in the 4th year of T'ien-c'hi, on the north bank of the Chwang river.*

有一個種田的人正在耕田碰見了玉璽 'yeu yih ko' chung' .t'ien tih .jen cheng' tsai' ,keng .t'ien p'eng' kien' 'liau yüh 'si, *an agricultural labourer as he was ploughing fell in with a jade seal.*

不敢自己藏着拿去送給本官 puh 'kan tsï' 'chi .t'sang choh 'na c'hü' sung' 'kei 'pen ,kwan, *he did not dare hide it, but took it to the mandarin of the place and presented it to him.*

四方的樣子橫的豎的四寸寬 sï' ,fang tih yang' 'tsï .heng tih shu' tih sï' t'sun' ,k'wan, *it was square in its form and was four inches wide, abroad and across.*

厚一寸二分 heu' yih t'sun' rï' ,fen, *it was in thickness an inch and two tenths.*

上面有龍頭叫做螭龍紐 shang' mien' 'yeu .lung .t'eu kiau' tso' .c'hï .lung 'nieu, *on its upper surface was a dragon shaped handle, called the crooked dragon button.*

螭龍紐高一寸八分 .c'hï .lung 'nieu ,kau yih t'sun' pah ,fen, *the crooked dragon button was one inch and eight tenths in height.*

頂要緊的是傳國玉璽從秦始皇朝代直傳到如今 'ting yau' 'chin tih shï' .c'hwen kweh yüh 'si .t'sung .T'sin 'shï .hwang .c'hau tai' chïh .c'hwen tau' .ju ,chin, *the most important is the seal for transmitting the empire, which from the reign of the emperor Tsin-shï-hwang has been preserved till the present time.*

皇帝賓天把傳國玉璽就傳給新皇帝 .hwang ti' ,pin ,t'ien pa' .c'hwen kweh yüh 'si, tsieu' .c'hwen kih ,sin .hwang ti', *the emperor when dying (when departing for heaven) takes the seal of hereditary government and gives it to the new emperor.*

LESSON 47. GRATITUDE, AN ANECDOTE.

遭難 'Tsau nan', *fall into misfortune.* [*fering.*
脫難 T'oh nan'; *escape suf-*
推給 T'ui 'kei, *to give away.*
奉事 Feng' shï', *to serve.*
郎中 .Lang ,chung, *member of a board.*
報恩 Pau' .ngen, *be grateful.*
收留 .Sheu .lieu, *to retain.*
官爵 ,Kwan tsioh, *government offices.*
一共 Yih kung', *the whole.*
皇上 .Hwang shang', *emperor.*
承認 .C'heng jen', *not to acknowledge.*
必定 Pih ting', *certainly.*

李大亮遭了難 Li' ta' liang' 'tsau 'liau nan', *Li-ta-liang fell into misfortune.*

張弼一個朋友救他的難, Chang pih yih ko' .p'eng 'yeu chieu' ,t'a tih nan', *Chang-pih a friend rescued him from trouble.*

後來發了富貴 heu' .lai fah 'liau fu' kwei', *afterwards he become rich and great.*

道上遇見張弼 tau' shang' ü' chien' ,Chang pih, *on the road he met Chang-pih.*

拉着他的手哭 ,la choh ,t'a tih 'sheu k'uh, *he seized him by the hand and wept.*

一切的家財全推給他 yih t'sieh' tih ,chia .t'sai .t'siuen ,t'ui kih ,t'a, *the whole of his property he gave over to him.* [*receive it.*

他不肯收留 ,t'a puh 'k'eng ,sheu .lieu, *he would not*
上朝說給皇帝聽 shang' .c'hau shwoh kih .hwang ti' ,t'ing, *going to court he related his story to the emperor.*

說道臣如今奉事皇上都是張弼的力量 shwoh tau' .c'hen .ju ,kin feng' sï' .hwang shang' ,tu shï' ,Chang pih tih lih liang', *he said, that your subject can at present serve the emperor is all due to the efforts of Chang-pih.*

情願把臣的官爵一共給他 .t'sing yuen' 'pa .c'hen tih ,kwan tsioh yih kung' kih ,t'a, *I desire that all my offices may be given to him.*

皇帝用他爲郎中 .hwang ti' yung', t'a .wei .lang ,chung, *the emperor employed him as a member of one of the boards.*

兩個人各有好處 liang' ko' .jen koh 'yeu 'hau c'hu', *the two men were both to be admired.*

這一個不承認自己有好處 che' yih ko' puh .c'heng jen' tsï' 'chi 'yeu 'hau c'hu', *the one would not admit that he was good.*

那一個必定要報恩 na' yih ko' pih ting' yau' pau' ,ngen, *the other was bent on recompensing a favour.*

LESSON 48. GENEROSITY, AN ANECDOTE.

諡法 .Sï fah, *posthumous title.*
王 .Wang, *king; royal title.*
公 ,Kung, *first title of nobility.*
共總 Kung' 'tsung, *altogether.*
升 ,Sheng, *one pint.*
回答 .Hwei tah, *to reply.*
次夜 T'sï' ye', *stay the night.*
挪動 .No tung', *to remove.*
公子 ,Kung 'tsï, *young gentleman.*
斛 Huh, *five teu.*
斗 'Teu, *ten pints*
了不得 'Liau puh teh, *extremely.*

宋朝有個宰相姓范的 Sung' .c'hau 'yeu ko' tsai' siang' sing' Fan' tih, *in the Sung dynasty there was a prime minister of the Fan family.*

諡法叫文正公 .Sï fah kiau' .Wen cheng' ,kung, *in his posthumous title he is styled the polished and correct noble of the first degree.*

打發他的兒子到蘇州去 'ta fah ,t'a tih .rï 'tsï tau', Su ,cheu c'hü', *he sent his son to Sucheu.*

將麥船拉回來 ,tsiang meh .c'hwen ,la .hwei .lai, *to bring back some boat loads of wheat.*

次夜在丹陽 t'sï' ye' tsai', Tan .yang, *he passed the night at Tan-yang.*

遇見一個老相好與父親同年的 ü' chien' yih ko' 'lau ,siang 'hau 'ü fu' ,t'sin .t'ung .nien tih, *he saw an old friend, of the same year with his father.*

說家裏三口人死了棺材不能挪動 shwoh ,chia 'li ,san 'k'eu .jen 'sï 'liau ,kwan .t'sai puh .neng .no tung', *who said that three persons of his family had died, and he had not yet been able to remove their coffins.*

葬好了回到北邊去 tsang' 'hau 'liau .hwei tau' peh pien' c'hü', *after they were buried, he would return to the north.*

沒有法子給他辦 muh 'yeu fah 'tsï kih ,t'a pan', *he had no means of doing any thing for him.*

無可奈何 .wu 'k'o nai' .ho, *there was nothing he could do.*

范公子就把麥船上帶來的麥子送了他 Fan' ,kung 'tsï tsieu' 'pa meh .c'hwen shang' tai' .lai tih meh 'tsï sung' 'liau ,t'a, *the young gentleman Fan then took the wheat on the boats and gave it him.*

共總有五百斛 kung' 'tsung 'you 'wu peh huh, *in all there were five hundred measures.*

回來他老子問他見過了什麼朋友沒有 .hwei .lai ,t'a 'lau 'tsï wen' ,t'a chien' kwo' 'liau shïh 'mo .p'eng 'you muh 'you, *on returning his father asked him if he had seen any friends or not?*

他告訴他老子在丹陽遇見了一個家中死了三口人的 ,t'a kau' su' ,t'a 'lau 'tsï tsai' ,Tan .yang ü' chien' 'liau yih ko' ,chia ,chung 'sï 'liau ,san 'k'eu .jen tih, *he told his father that at Tan-yang he had met one who had had three persons of his family die.*

他老子聽見他說就問為什麼不把船上的麥子幫他 ,t'a 'lau 'tsï ,t'ing chien' shwoh tsieu' wen' ,t'a wei' shïh 'mo puh 'pa .c'hwen shang' tih meh 'tsï ,pang ,t'a, *his father hearing what he said, at once asked him why he did not give him the wheat in the boats to assist him.*

他回答說我已經把船上的麥子送了他 ,t'a .hwei tah shwoh 'wo 'i ,ching 'pa .c'hwen shang' tih meh 'tsï sung' 'liau ,t'a, *he replied, I have already presented him with the wheat on the boats.*

他老子聽見了喜歡的了不得 ,t'a 'lau 'tsï ,t'ing chien' 'liau 'hi ,hwan tih 'liau puh teh, *his father on hearing it was extremely pleased.*

LESSON 49. SELF-CONTROL, AN ANECDOTE.

從前有個宰相姓韓的死了後封他做了魏國公 .ts'ung .ts'ien 'you ko' tsai' siang' sing' Han' ,tih[*] 'sï 'liau heu' ,feng ,t'a tso' 'liau .Wei kwëh ,kung, *formerly*

---

[*] From this lesson onwards the Peking sounds are given for words in juh sheng, but the distinguishing *h* final used for all words in this tone-class is retained.

there was a prime minister whose family name was Han; after his death he was honoured with the title Wei kweh kung, i. e. noble of the first rank of the kingdom of Wei.

他家裏收着一個玉酒杯 ,t'a ,chia 'li ,sheu .choh ,yih ko' yüh' 'tsieu .pei, in his house he had a jade-stone wine-cup. [indeed an invaluable treasure.

眞是無價之寶 ,chen shï' .wu ,chia ,chï 'pau, it was

每次請客飲酒必要拿出來擱在席上 'mei t'sï' 't'sing k'eh' 'yin 'tsieu .pih yau' .na ,ch'uh .lai ,koh tsai' .sih shang', every time he invited guests to drink wine it was constantly brought out to place on the table.

最是他心愛的東西 tsui' shï' ,t'a ,sin ngai' ,tih ,tung ,si, it was a thing exceedingly valued.

那一天教底下人摔了個細碎 na' yih' ,t'ien chiau' 'ti hia' .jen ,shwaih 'liau ko' si' sui', one day by a servant it was thrown down and broken into small pieces.

把底下人嚇的臉上都改了顏色 pa' 'ti hia' .jen hiah' ,tih 'lien shang' ,tu 'kai 'liau .yen .'shih, the servant was so frightened that his face quite lost its colour.

跪在地下磕頭問該治他甚麽罪 kwei' tsai' ti' hia' ,k'oh .t'eu wen' ,kai chï' ,t'a shen' 'mo tsui', he knelt down and knocked his head on the ground asking what punishment should be adjudged him.

魏國公向他一瞧 .Wei kwèh ,kung hiang' ,t'a ,yih .t'siau, the chief noble of the Wei kingdom glanced at him.

不慌不忙的告訴他說 puh' ,hwang puh' .mang ,tih kau' su' ,t'a ,shwoh, without haste or agitation, he spoke to him as follows,—

無論甚麽東西該成該破都有一定的氣數 .wu lun' shen' 'mo ,tung ,si ,kai .ch'eng ,kai p'o' ,tu 'yeu ,yih ting' ,tih ch'i' shu', every thing no matter what, whether it is to be preserved or broken has a fixed destiny.

况且你是一時失手 k'wang' ,t'sie 'ni shï' ,yih .shï ,shïh 'sheu, and more than this you have for once let it fall.

並非故意的要匜破他 ping' ,fei ku'i' ,tih yau' .tsa p'o' ,t'a, it certainly is not wilfully that you desired to break it.

說着臉上並沒有一點惱怒的意思和尋常

一樣 ,shwoh ,choh 'lien shang' ping' .muh 'yeu yih' 'tien 'nau nu' ,tih i' ,sï .ho .siün .c'hang .yih yang', *as he spoke on his contenance there was not any appearance of anger, it looked the same as it ordinarily did.*

連責備責備都不忍的 .lien .tseh pei' .tseh pei' ,tu ,puh jen' ,tih, *as to reproving, he could not bear to reprove.*

LESSON 50. INTEGRITY, AN ANECDOTE.

中國念書人有一個叫司馬溫公,Chung .kweh nien' ,shu .jen 'yeu .yih ko' chiau' ,Sï .ma ,wen ,kung, *among the literary men of China is one called Sï-ma Wen-kung, or the gentle noble of the Sï-ma family.*

在家裏蓋了一個花園為的是自己行樂就叫獨樂園 tsai' ,chia 'li kai' 'liau .yih ko' ,hwa .yuen .wei ,tih shï' tsï' 'chi .hing loh' tsieu' chiau' .tuh loh' yuen, *at his residence he built a flower garden, and because it was for his own enjoyment, he called it the garden of solitary pleasure.*

有個看園子的人名叫呂直 'yeu ko' k'an' .yuen 'tsï ,tih .jen .ming chiau' 'Lü .chïh, *there was a gardener there of the Lü family, called Straight-forward.*

因為他性子愚魯做出事來不會灣灣轉轉的 ,yin wei' ,t'a sing' 'tsï .ü 'lu tso' ,c'huh shï' .lai .puh hwei' ,wan ,wan 'chwen 'chwen ,tih, *because his disposition was simple and rude, and he could not do things in a crooked manner.*

溫公就給他起了一個直字的名字,Wen ,kung tsieu' keih ,t'a 'c'hi 'liau .yih ko' .chïh tsï' ,tih .ming tsï', *Wen-kung on this account choose for him the character Chïh as his name, meaning "Straight-forward." [when spring arrived.*

到了春天的時候 tau' 'liau ,c'hun ,t'ien ,tih .shï heu', 有讀書的人三五成羣都到園裏來遊玩 'yeu .tuh ,shu ,tih .jen ,san 'wu .c'heng .c'hiün .,tu tau' .yuen 'li .lai .yeu wan', *many students of books, in companies of three and five, came to the garden to walk about for pleasure.*

看園子的得的茶錢不少數了一數就有十吊都是他們留下的 k'an' .yuen 'tsï ,tih .teh ,tih .c'ha

.t'sien puh‘ 'shau shu‘ 'liau .yih shu‘ tsieu‘ 'yeu .shïh tiau‘ ,tu shï‘ ,t'a .men .lieu hia‘ ,tih, *the gardener received tea-money to no small amount, and after counting it found that he had ten strings (about £2.10 of our money) which had been left by them.*

那一天看園子的呂直把這十吊錢一五一十交給溫公 na‘ yih‘ ,t'ien k'an‘ .yuen 'tsï .tih 'Lü .chih pa‘ che‘ ,shïh tiau‘ .t'sien yih‘ 'wu yih‘ .shïh ,chiau 'kei ,Wen ,kung, *that very day the gardener Lü-chih took these ten strings of cash, and in fives and tens gave them to Wen-kung.*

溫公說這是你應該得的錢 ,Wen ,kung ,shwoh che‘ shï‘ 'ni 'ing ,kai‘ teh ,tih .t'sien, *Wen-kung said, this money you ought to receive.*

拿了去罷 .na 'liau c'hü‘ pa‘, *take it and go.*

說了幾遍他一定要留下 ,shwoh 'liau 'chi pien‘ ,t'a .yih ting‘ yau‘ lieu hia‘, *after repeating it several times, he still insisted on leaving it.*

惹的溫公都惱了 'je .tih ,Wen ,kung ,tu 'nau 'liau, *until he provoked Wen-kung to become angry.*

纔勉強拿了去 .t'sai 'mien 'c'hiang .na 'liau c'hü‘, *he then reluctantly carried it away.*

還回着頭說只有主人不愛錢麼 .hwan .hwei ,choh .t'eu ,shwoh .chïh 'yeu 'chu .jen .puh ngai‘ .t'sien 'mo, *turning his head round he said, it is only my master I suppose that does not love money?*

又過了十幾天 yeu‘ kwo‘ 'liau .shïh 'chi ,t'ien, *again a few days passed away.*

主人到園裏見井上新蓋了一個亭子 'chu .jen tau‘ .yuen 'li chien‘ 'tsing shang‘ ,sin kai‘ 'liau .yih ko‘ .t'ing 'tsï, *the master going into his garden saw over the well a new arbour erected.*

盤問他們 .p'an wen‘ ,t'a .men, *he asked those who were* [*there respecting it.*

纔知道就是前日看園子得的那十吊錢新蓋的 .t'sai ,chï-tau‘ tsieu‘ shï‘ .t'sien jïh‘ k'an‘ .yuen 'tsï .teh ,tih na‘ .shïh tiau‘ .t'sien ,sin kai‘ ,tih, *he then learned that it was newly built with the ten strings of cash obtained by the gardener.*

LESSON 51. RULES FOR A FREE-SCHOOL.

設立義學必須請人品端正人的做先生 shèh‘ lih‘ i‘ .hiöh pih‘, sü‘ t'sing jen 'p'in, twan cheng‘, tih .jen tso‘, sien ,sheng, *in establishing a charity school, you must invite a man of upright character to be master.*

學文要通達教訓要盡心 .hiuèh .wen yau‘, t'ung .ta chiau‘ hiün‘ yau‘ tsin‘, sin, *in his learning he must be thorough, and in his teaching diligent and faithful.*

這個義學纔不致有名無實 che‘ ko‘ i‘ .hiuèh .t'sai .puh chï‘ 'yeu .ming .wu .shïh, *this charity school will then not become a name without reality.*

經管此事的人每年秋冬的時候兩下定見明白, ching 'kwan 't'sï shï‘, tih .jen 'mei .nien ,t'sieu ,tung, tih .shï heu‘ liang‘ hia‘ ting‘ chien‘ .ming .peh, *those who superintend the matter, every year in the autumn or winter, make the arrangements on both sides.*

開館的日子前三天用紅帖奉請先生來 ,k‘ai 'kwan ,tih jïh‘ 'tsï .t'sien ,san ,t'ien yung‘ .hung ,t'ieh ,fung 't'sing ,sien ,sheng .lai, *three days before the time of opening the school, a red card should be prepared and presented to the master inviting him to come.*

先生束脩一年二十八千文,sien ,sheng .suh ,sieu yih‘ .nien rï‘ .shïh ,pah ,t'sien .wen, *the master's emolument shall be twenty eight thousand cash in a year.*

飯錢點心錢每年共總二十八千文 fan‘ .t'sien 'tien ,sin .t'sien 'mei .nien kung‘ 'tsung rï‘ .shïh ,pah ,t'sien .wen, *his allowance for dinners and luncheons will be in all twenty eight thousand cash.*

學生七歲以上纔可以上學堂 .hiöh ,sheng ,t'sih sui‘ 'i shang‘ .t'sai 'k'o 'i shang‘ .hiöh .t'ang, *pupils of seven years and more can enter the school.*

他們的父親哥哥預先要開明本學生的姓名年紀住處送到學堂來好上薄子,t'a .men ,tih fu‘ ,t'sin ,ko ,ko yü‘ ,sien yau‘ ,k'ai .ming 'pen .hiöh ,sheng ,tih sing‘ .ming, .nien 'chi chu‘ c'hu‘ sung‘ tau‘ .hiöh .t'ang .lai 'hau shang‘ pu‘ 'tsï, *their fathers and elder* brothers must prepare a clear statement of the surnames and proper names, age and residence of the pupils, and bring it to the school that entries may be made on the books.

學生到館各人在帝君面前做三個揖 ,hiauh ,sheng tau‘ ‘kwan ‘koh ,jen tsai‘ ti‘ ,chiun mien‘ .t‘sien tso‘ ,san ko‘ ,yih, *the scholars on arriving at the school are to make three bows to the god of literature.* [take their seats.

後來就歸坐 heu‘ .lai tsieu‘ ,kwei tso‘, *after this they*
到夜裏放學的時候也照這樣 tau‘ ye‘ ‘li fang‘ .hioh ,tih .shï heu‘ ‘yo chau‘ che‘ yang‘, *at night when the school is dismissed they do this again.*

每月初一十五先生領他們到文帝武帝魁星面前做兩個揖 ’mei yuĕh‘ ,c‘hu ,yih .shïh ‘wu ,sien ,sheng ‘ling ,t‘a .men tau‘ .wen ti‘ ‘wu ti‘ ,k‘wei ,sing mien‘ .t‘sien tso‘ ‘liang ko‘ ,yih, *every month, on the first and fifteenth, the master is to take the pupils to make two bows before the gods of literature and military affairs and before K‘wei-sing (a star in the Great Bear).*

經管的人一個月兩次親自到館中 ,ching ’kwan ,tih ,jen ,yih ko‘ yuĕh‘ ‘liang t‘sï‘ ,t‘sin tsï‘ tau‘ ‘kwan ,chung, *the superintendents twice a month go themselves to the school.*

查問功課把他所念的書抽出一本來教他熟背 .c‘ha wen‘ ,kung k‘o pa‘ ,t‘a ‘so nien‘ ,tih ,shu ,c‘heu ,c‘huh yih‘ ’pen .lai chiau‘ ,t‘a .sheuh pei‘, *they inquire into the tasks of the pupils, take the books they read, select a volume, and call on them to recite it without mistake.*

所認的字指出幾個來教他識認 ’so jen‘ ,tih tsï‘ ‘chï ,c‘huh ‘chi ko‘ .lai chiau‘ ,t‘a ,shïh jen‘, *as to the characters the scholars know, they point them, and require their sound to be given.*

若是有背不過來和不認得字的 joh‘ shï‘ ‘yeu pei‘ .puh kwo‘ .lai .ho puh‘ jen‘ .teh tsï‘ ,tih, *if any one cannot recite, and does not know characters correctly.*

把他的姓名貼在牆上記過 ’pa ,t‘a ,tih sing‘ .ming t‘iĕh tsai‘ .t‘siang shang‘ chi‘ kwo‘, *his name is pasted on the wall to be remembered.*

三次不改請先生分別責打 ,san t'sï' puh' 'kai 't'sing ,sien ,sheng ,fen .pièh tseh ,ta, *after three times should he not improve, the master is desired to give him a proportional beating on the hand.*

背書熟認字眞寫字好的賞他買筆的錢 pei' ,shu .sheuh, ,jen' tsï' ,chen, 'sie tsï' 'hau ,tih, 'shang ,t'a 'mai .pih ,tih .t'sien, *if they recite their books perfectly, give the sound of the characters correctly, and write neatly, they are to be rewarded with cash to buy writing pencils.*

書館裏有大學生欺負小學生愛打架的趕他出去不准上館 ,shu 'kwan 'li 'yeu ta' .hioh ,sheng ,c'hi fu' 'siau .hioh ,sheng, ngai' 'ta chia' ,tih 'kan ,t'a c'huh c'hü', puh' 'chun shang' 'kwan, *if in the school any old scholar ill treat any young scholar, and if there be any who are fond of fighting, they must be driven from the school.*

LESSON 52. A CAVERN.

京西有雲水洞是有名的 ,king ,si 'yeu .Yün 'shui tung' shï' 'yeu .ming ,tih, *on the west of the capital, the Cloud and water cavern is celebrated.*

離着煤窰不遠在高山邊上 .li ,,choh .mei .yau puh' 'yuen tsai' ,kau ,shan ,pien shang', *it is not distant from the coal mines, and is on the side of a high hill.*

有和尚住在洞門替客人領路的 'yeu .ho shang' chu' tsai' tung' .men t̯ï' k'eh' .jen 'ling lu' ,tih, *there is a priest who lives at the door of the cavern, who leads the way for visitors.*

帶着火把走進去 tai' ,choh 'hwo 'pa 'tseu tsin' c'hü', *taking torches they enter.*

裏面的石頭彷彿滴水成的冰 'li mien', ,tih .shih .t'eu 'fang fuh' ,tih 'shui .c'heng ,tih ,ping, *the stone within, is like dropping water forming icicles.*

這個洞有口叫做牛郞口矮得狠總要扒着進去 cho' ko' tung' 'yeu 'k'eu chiau' tso' .nieu .lang 'k'eu ngai' teh 'hen 'tsung yau' .p'a ,choh tsin' c'hü', *this cavern has a passage called the herdsman's passage, it is very low; you must creep to pass through it.*

一路進去景致狠多 .yih luʻ tsinʻ cʻhüʻ ʻking chïʻ ʻhen ,to, *all the way in, the curiosities are very numerous.*

有兩條石龍把守着洞口 ʻyeu ʻliang .tʻiau .shïh .lung ʻpa ʻsheu ,choh tungʻ ʻkʻeu, *there are two stone dragons guarding the cavern entrance.*

有黑龍潭是乾的白龍潭是有水的 ʻyeu ,hei .lung .tʻan shï ,kan ,tih .pai .lung .tʻan shï ʻyeu ʻshui ,tih, *there is also a black dragon pool, which is dry, and a white dragon pool with water.*

又有拴虎樁 yeuʻ ʻyeu ,shwen ʻhu ,chwang, *there is also a pillar called the tiger-tying post.*

把火把照着光 ʻpa ʻhwo ʻpa chaouʻ ,choh ,kwang, *take a torch and shew a light.*

當初有人到洞裏來尋找寶石 tang ,chʻu ʻyeu .jen tauʻ tungʻ .li .lai .siün ʻchau ʻpau .shïh, *formerly a man went into the cavern to seek for precious stones.*

不知甚麼緣故他就死了 puhʻ ,chï shenʻ ʻmo .yuen kuʻ ,tʻa tsieuʻ ʻsï ʻliau, *I do not know what was the cause of it, but he died there.*

水滴在他的身上漸漸的成了石頭 ʻshui ,tih fsaiʻ ,tʻa ,tih ,shen shangʻ ,tsien ,tsien ,tih .cʻheng ʻliau .shïh .tʻeu, *water dropped on his body and gradually he was turned into stone.*

如今躺在洞裏面伏着地 ju ,chin ,tʻang tsaiʻ tungʻ ʻli mienʻ ,fuh ,choh tiʻ, *he is now lying in the cavern with his face to the ground.*

這石頭人叫做回回別寶 cheʻ .shïh .tʻeu .jen chiauʻ tsoʻ .hwei .hwei .pièh ʻpau, *this stone man is called the Mahometan selecting precious stones.*

進去八里路有水 tsinʻ cʻhüʻ ,pah ʻli luʻ ʻyeu ʻshui, *after entering for a distance of eight li there is water.*

和尚早把木頭做了个柵欄不叫人進去又遠 .ho shangʻ ʻtsau ʻpaʻ muhʻ ,tʻeu tsoʻ ʻliau koʻ chahʻ .lan puhʻ chiauʻ .jen tsinʻ cʻhüʻ yeuʻ ʻyuen, *the priests early made a wooden barrier to prevent persons going farther.*

嘉慶年間有兩個人進去沒有出來 ,chia cʻhingʻ

.nien ,chien 'yeu 'liang ko‘ ,jen tsin‘ c‘hü‘ mei‘ 'yeu c‘huh .lai, *in the reign of Kia-k'ing (about 50 years since) two men entered who never came out again.*

LISTS OF USEFUL WORDS AND SHORT PHRASES.

1. *Place and Direction.*

裏面 'li mien‘, *inside.*
外頭 wai‘ .t‘eu, *outside.*
城裏 .c‘heng 'li, *in the city.*
城外 .c‘heng wai‘, *outside the city.*
橋上 .c‘hiau shang‘, *on the bridge.*
樓上 .leu shang‘, *up stairs.*
京西 ,ching ,si, *west of the capital.*
宮北 ,kung 'pei, *north of the temple.*
鼓樓東 'ku .leu ,tung, *east of the drum tower.*
底下 'ti hia‘, *under.*
脚底下 'chiauh 'ti hia‘, *under foot.*
這邊 che‘ ,pien, *on this side.*
那邊 na‘ ,pien, *on that side.*
廟前 miau‘ .t‘sien, *before the temple.*
不在 puh‘ tsai‘, *not at home.*
在家 tsai‘ ,chia, 在 tsai‘, *at home.*
這塊兒 che‘ k‘wai‘ .rï, 這兒 che‘ .hai .rï, *here.*
在內 tsai‘ nei‘, 內中 nei‘ ,chung, *among them.*
對面 tui‘ mien‘, 對過 tui‘ kwo‘, *opposite.*
各處 koh‘ c‘hu‘, *everywhere.*
南邊 .nan ,pien, *on the south.*
周圍 ,cheu .wei, 四面 sï‘ mien‘, *all round.*
踒彎兒 kwai‘ wan .rï, *obliquely.*
北山 'peih ,shan, *northern mountains.*
西湖 ,si .hu, *west lake.*
往東走 'wang ,tung 'tseu, *go to the east.*
一直 yih‘ .chïh, *straight.*
遶着走 jau‘ cho 'tseu, *to go round.*

那裏 'na 'li, *where?*
那裏 na‘ 'li, 那兒 na‘ .rĭ, *there.*
那一條道 'na yih‘ .t‘iau, tau‘, *which road?*
這裏來 che‘ 'li .lai, *come here.*
心中 ,sin ,chung, *in the heart.*

2. Time.

今日 ,chin jih‘, 今兒 ,chin .rĭ, *to-day.*
明日 .ming jih‘, 明兒 .ming .rĭ, *to-morrow.*
昨日 .tsoh jih‘, 昨兒 .tsoh .rĭ, *yesterday.*
今天 ,chin ,t‘ien, *to-day.*
明天 .ming ,t‘ien, *to-morrow.*
後日 heu‘ jih‘, 後天 heu‘ ,t‘ien, *day after to-morrow.*
如今 .ju ,chin, 現今 hien‘ ,chin, *now.*
當下 ,tang hia‘, 當現 ,tang hien‘, *now.*
後來 heu‘ .lai, *afterwards.*
先要 ,sien yau, *you must first.*
末後兒 moh‘ heu‘ .rĭ, 末後 moh‘ heu‘, *afterwards; at last.*
偶然 'ngeu .jan, 偶兒 'ngeu .rĭ, *occasionally.*
尋常 .siün .c‘hang, 常常 .c‘hang .c‘hang, *constantly.*
正 cheng‘, 正在 cheng‘ tsai‘, *just as; just at.*
纔剛 .t‘sai ,kang, 纔 .t‘sai, *just now.*
剛纔 ,kang .t‘sai, 剛剛 ,kang ,kang, 剛 ,kang, *just now.*
就說 tsieu‘ ,shwo, *he then said.*
每年 ,mei .nien, *every year.*
一次 .yih t‘sĭ‘, *once.*
忽然 hwuh‘ .jan, *suddenly.*
已經 'i ,ching, *already.*
去年 c‘hü‘ .nien, *last year.*
明年 .ming .nien, *next year.*
隔三天 .keh ,san .t‘ien, *after three days.*
正月 ,cheng yueh‘, *first month.*
臘月 lah‘ yueh‘, *twelfth month.*
下午 hia‘ ,wu, *in the afternoon.*

再說 tsai' shwo', *say it again.*
三日後再來 ,san jĭh' heu' ,tsai .lai, *come again after three days.*
二月裏 rï' yuèh' 'li, *in the second month.*
幾點鐘 'chi 'tien ,chung, 幾下鐘 'chi hia',chung, *what is the hour?*
幾時 'chi .shï, *what time?*
一個禮拜 .yih ko' 'li .pai', *one week.*
半個月 pan' ko' yuèh', *half a month.*
一年半 yih' .nien pan', *a year and a half.*
二更天 rï' ,keng (i) ,t'ien, *the second watch.*
初一 ,c'hu .yih, *the first day of the month.* [cade.]
初幾 ,c'hu 'chi, *what day of the month it is?* (in the first de-
十幾 .shĭh 'chi, *what day of the month?* (in the second decade.)
二十幾 rï' .shĭh 'chi, *do.* (in the 3rd decade.)

3. *Affirmative and Negative Expressions.*

有 'yeu, 有的 'yeu ,tih, *there is; there are.*
沒有 .mei 'yeu, *there is none; there are none.*
着 ,cho, *it is so; yes.*
有呢 'yeu 'ni, *is there any?*
是的 shï' ,tih, 是 shï', *yes ; it is so.*
不錯 puh' t'soh', *it is not wrong; it is so.*
不是 puh' shï', *it is not so.*
可以 'ko 'i, *you may; it will do.*
差不多 ,c'ha puh' ,to, *it differs little.*
不離 puh' .li, *it is not far from it.*
差遠 ,c'ha 'yuen, *it is very different.*
狠是 'hen shï', *it is very true.*
總要 'tsung yau', *you must.*
總是 'tsung shï', *it must be...*
就是 tsieu' shï', *it is just...*
纔是 .t'sai shï', *it is then correct.*
原是 .yuen shï', *it is as before.*
不拘 puh' ,chü, *it matters not which.*
不准 puh' 'chun, *it is not certain.*

不定 puh' ting', *it is not certain.*
有趣 'yeu 't'sü, *it is pretty; it is well.*
沒趣 .mei 't'sü, *it is not pretty; it is not well.*
不必 puh' 'pih, *you need not.*
可不是 'k'o puh' shï', *it is not so?*
不同 puh' .t'ung, *not the same.*
不通 puh' ,t'ung, *not reasonable.*
不行 puh' .hing, *it will not do.*
不對 puh' tui', *it does not agree.*
無論 .wu lun', *without considering.*
不配 puh' p'ei', *ought not; not a match for.*
不敢 puh' 'kan, *not dare.*
不止 puh' 'chï, *does not stop; not only.*
不關 puh' ,kwan, *it does not concern.*
並不是 ping' puh' shï', *it certainly is not.*
不懂 puh' 'tung, *I do not understand.*
不肯 puh' 'k'en, *not willing; I will not.*
不到本 puh' tau' 'pen, *not so much as I gave for it.*

4. *Common Adjectives.*

大 ta', *great,* 小 'siau, *little.*
多 ,to, *many,* 少 'shau, *few.*
乾 ,kan *dry,* 濕 ,shïh, *wet; moist.*
淨 tsing', *clean,* 髒 'tsang, *dirty.*
高 ,kau, *high,* 低 ,ti, *low.*
寬 ,k'wan, *wide,* 窄 'chaih, *narrow.*
軟 'jwan, *soft.* 硬 ying', *hard.*
窮 .c'hiung, *poor.* 富 fu', *rich.*
橫的 .heng ,tih, *across;* 竪的 shu' ,tih, *upright.*
涼 .liang, *cold,* 熱 joh', *hot.*
快 k'wai', *quick,* 慢 man', *slow.*
現成的 hien' .c'heng ,tih, *ready-made; ready.*
定做的 ting' tso' ,tih, *made to order.*
厚 heu', *thick,* 薄 .pauh, *thin.*
甜 .t'ien, *sweet,* 酸 ,suan, *sour.*
苦 'k'u, *bitter;* 辣 la', *hot.*

省錢的 'sheng .t'sien ,tih, *economical.*
費錢的 fei' .t'sien ,tih, *wasteful in expenditure.*
好 'hau, *good,* 不好 puh' 'hau, *bad.*
四方的 sï' ,fang ,tih, *square.*
平常 .p'ing .c'hang, *common.*
黑 hei, *black; dark,* 白 .pai, *white.*
暗 ngan', *dark,* 亮 liang', *bright.*
生 ,sheng, *raw; strange,* 熟 .sheu, *ripe; cooked.*
長 .c'hang, *long,* 短 'twan, *short.*
貴 kwei', *dear; honourable,* 賤 tsien', *cheap; mean.*
深 ,shen, *deep,* 淺 't'sien, *shallow.*
冷 'leng, *cold,* 暖 .nwan, *warm.*
早 'tsau, *early,* 晚 wan', *late.*
新 .sin, *new,* 舊 chieu', *old.*
鬆 ,sung, *loose; easy; light,* 緊 'chin, *tight.*
真 ,chen, *true,* 假 'chia, *false.*
老實 'lau .shïh, *honest,* 結實 .chieh .shïh, *firm.*
謙虛 ,c'hien ,hü, *humble,* 驕傲 ,chiau ngau', *proud.*
聰明 ,t'sung .ming, *intelligent,* 笨 pen', *stupid.*
便當 pien' ,tang, *convenient.*
整 'cheng, *entire,* 雜亂 .tsa lan', *confused.*
利害 li' hai', *dangerous.*
重 chung', *heavy,* 輕 ,c'hing, *light.*
清白 ,c'hing .paih, *plain; intelligible.*
難得 .nan .toh, *rare,* 容易 .yung i', *easy.*

5. *Prepositions.*

和 .ho, .hwan, .hai, *and; with.*
連 .lien, *together with.* 同 .t'ung, 幷 ping', *with.*
到 tau', *to.*
打 'ta, 從 .t'sung, *from.* 由 .yeu, *from; by.*
替 t'i', *on behalf of.* 代 tai', *for.*
在 tsai', *at; to be at.*
向 hiang', *towards; to.*
根 ,ken, *with (as a conjunction such as and).*

當 ,tang, *before,* as in 當我面前 ,tang 'wo mien' .t'sien,
對 tui', *towards, in correspondence with.* [*before my face.*
爲 wei', *for; in account of.*
給 'kei, *for; to give to.* Read chi', *to give.*
因 ,yin, as 因爲 ,yin wei', *because of.*

6. *Postpositions.*

裡 'li, *in,* as in 衙門裡 .ya .men 'li, *in the magistrate's*
前 .t'sien, *before,* 跟前 'ken .t'sien. [*office.*
中 ,chung, *in,* as in 內中 nei' ,chung, *among them.*
後 heu', *behind,* 門後 .men heu', *behind the door.*
上 shang', *upon,* as 身上 ,shen shang', *on the person.*
下 hia', *under,* as 手下 'sheu hia', *under the hand.*
外 wai', *outside,* as in 門外 .men wai', *outside the door.*
內 nei', *inside,* as in 心內 ,sin nei', *in the heart.*

7. *Fragmentary Clauses at the end of Sentences.*

就完 tsieu' .wan, *and that will be sufficient.*
便罷 pien' pa', *then let it be so.*
纔好 .t'sai 'hau, *it is then all well.*
纔知道 .t'sai ,chï tau', *and then you will know.*
不成 puh' .c'heng, *an interrogative of remonstrance.*
就罷 tsieu' pa', *then let it be so.*

8. *Conjunctions.*

但 tan', 但是 tan' shï', *but.*
得閒呢 .teh .hien ,ni, *if he is at leisure.*
連說話也不能 .lien ,shwoh hwa' 'ye puh' .neng, *he could not even speak.*
不好的人又多 puh' 'hau ,tih .jen 'yeu' ,to, *and bad men are numerous.*
倒不比從前 'tau puh' 'pi .t'sung .t'sien, *yet it is not to be compared with the past.*
更有一種 ,keng 'yeu yih' 'chung, *there is also another sort.*
雖然懊悔也是遲了 ,sui .jan .ngau 'hwei 'ye shï' .chï 'liau, *although you should repent, yet it is too late.*
連吃帶飲 ,lien c'hï tai' ,hoh, *both eating and drinking.*

若是再不肯的 joh' shï' tsai' puh' 'k'en ,tih, *if again*
就是 tsieu' shï', *even if; but even.* [*you are not willing.*
不獨 puh' .tuh, *not only* .... 連 .lien, *but also* ....
萬一就做不出來 wan' yih' tsieu' tso' puh' ,c'huh .lai, *even if he can in no case do it.*
一面走一面笑 yih' mien' 'tseu yih' mien' 'siau, *he both walked and smiled, or he walked on smiling.*
還是過路還是特來的 .hwan shï' ,kwo lu' .hwan shï' t'eh' .lai ,tih, *whether you are passing, or have come on purpose.*
不知可用了飯沒有 puh' ,chï 'k'o yung' 'liau fan' muh 'yeu, *I do not know whether they have dined or not?*
寧死不敢 .ning 'sï puh' 'kan, *rather die than dare do it.*
求也無益 .c'hieu 'ye .wu .yih, *entreating is also of no use.*
一會兒開着一會兒關着 yih' 'hwei .rï ,k'ai ,choh yih' 'hwei .rï ,kwan ,choh, *for a moment he opened it and then in a moment he closed it.*
還 .hwan, .han or .hai, *and* 還有一樣 .hai 'yeu ,yih yang', *and there is another thing.*
並且 ping' 't'sie, *and further.*
尚且 shang' 't'sie, *and if further.*
也深也清 'ye ,shen 'ye ,t'sing, *both deep and clear.*
倒 'tau, *but,* 也 'ye, *but, and* 說要來倒不來 ,shwoh yau' .lai 'tau puh' .lai, *he said he would come but did not.*
也 'ye, *but, and* 你去也更好 'ni c'hü' 'ye ,keng 'hau, *but it would be better for you to go.*
因此 ,yin t'sï', 所以 'so 'i, *therefore.*
因爲 ,yin .wei, *because,* 爲的是 wei' ,tih shï', *because.*
教他 chiau' ,t'a, 要他 yau' ,t'a, *in order that he, or so that he* ---
恐怕 'k'ung p'a', *lest.*
倘或 't'ang hoh', *if,* 倘便 't'ang shï', *if.*
若是 joh' shï' or yau' shï', *if.*
旣然 chi' ,jan, *if it be already so.*

9. *Names of Imported articles, Wax, etc.*

日本臘 jih' 'pen lah', *Japan wax.*

蘇合油 ,su .hoh .yeu, *storax.*
硝 ,siau, *saltpetre.*
黃臘 .hwang lah', *yellow bees' wax.*
硫黃 .lieu .hwang, *sulphur.*

10. *Imports, Incense, Pepper, etc.*

安息香 ,ngan ,sih ,hiang, *gum benjamin.*
安息油 ,ngan ,sih .yeu, *oil of gum benjamin.*
檀香 .t'an ,hiang, *sandal-wood.*
白棚椒 .paih .hu ,tsiau, *white pepper.*
黑棚椒 ,heih .hu ,tsiau, *black pepper.*
沉香 .c'hen ,hiang, *garroo-wood.*
降香 chiang' ,hiang, *lakka-wood.*

11. *Imported Medicines.*

阿魏 ,ngo .wei, *assafœtida.*
上冰片 shang' ,ping p'ien', *clean baroos camphor.*
下冰片 hia' ,ping p'ien', *refuse baroos camphor.*
丁香 ,ting ,hiang, *cloves.*
母丁香 'mu ,ting ,hiang, *mother cloves.*
印度牛黃 yin' tu' ,nieu .hwang, *Indian cow bezoar.*
兒茶 .ri ,.c'ha, *cutch.*
檳榔膏 ,ping .lang 'kau, *betel-nut cake.*
檳榔 ,ping .lang, *betel-nut.*
美國參 'mei .kwoh shen', or 西參 ,si shen', *American ginseng.*
揀淨參鬚參 'chien tsing' shen', sü shen', *the ginseng root denuded of its hairy appendage.*
乳香 .ju ,hiang, *olibanum, gum resin,* or *frankincense.*
沒藥 moh' yauh', *myrrh.*
荳蔻花 'teu k'eu' ,hwa, *nutmeg flowers.*
肉果 juh' 'kwo or 肉荳蔻 juh' 'teu k'eu', *nutmegs.*
白荳蔻 .paih 'teu k'eu', *rose mallows.*
木香 muh' ,hiang, *putchuck.*
犀角 ,si 'chiau, *rhinoceros horns.*

水銀 'shui .yin, *quicksilver*.
洋藥 .yang yauh', *opium*.
梹榔衣 ,ping .lang ,i, *husks of betel-nut*.
肉桂 juh' kwei', *cinnamon*.
虎骨 'hu ,ku, *tiger's bones*.
鹿角 luh' 'chiau, *deer horns*.
血竭 'hiuèh .chièh, *dragon's blood gum*.
大楓子 ta' ,feng 'tsī, *lucraban seed*.

12. Imported Miscellaneous articles.

火石 'hwo .shih, *flints*.
雲母殼 .yün 'mu 'c'hian, *mother of pearl shell*.
銅鈕扣 .t'ung 'nieu k'ou', *brass buttons*.
漆器 ,c'hi c'hi', *lacquered ware*.
呂宋繩 'lü ,sung .sheng, *Manila cordage*.
傘 san', *umbrellas*.
香柴 ,hiang .c'hai, *fragrant wood*.
外國煤 wai' .kwoh .mei, *foreign coal*.
火絨 'hwo .jung, *tinder*.

13. Imported Marine productions.

上燕窩 shang' yen' ,wo, *birds' nests, 1st quality*.
中燕窩 ,chung yen' ,wo, *birds' nests, 2nd quality*.
下燕窩 hia' yen' ,wo, *birds' nests, 3rd quality*.
黑海參 ,heih 'hai shen', *black bicho-de-mar*.
白海參 .paih 'hai shen', *white bicho-de-mar*.
白魚翅 .paih .yü c'hï, *white sharks' fins*.
黑魚翅 ,heih .yü c'hï, *black sharks' fins*.
乾魚 ,kan .yü, or 柴魚 .c'hai .yü, *stock fish*.
魚肚 .yü tu', *fish maws*.
鹹魚 .hien .yü, *salt fish*.
魚皮 .yü .p'i, *fish skins*.
海菜 'hai t'sai', *agar agar; an edible fungus*.
牛鹿筋 .nieu luh' ,chin, *buffalo and deer sinews*.
蝦米 ,hia 'mi, *dried prawns*.

淡菜 tan‘ t‘sai‘, *dried mussels.*
鯊魚皮 ,sha .yü .p‘i, *shark skins.*

14, Imported Dyeing and Colouring materials.

呀嚂米 ,ya .lan 'mi, *cochineal.*
大青 ta‘ ,t‘sing, *gambier; a mineral green.*
蘇木 ,su muh‘, *sapan-wood.*
紫梗 'tsï ,k‘eng, *sticklac; a vegetable medicine.*
水靛 'shui tian‘, *liquid indigo.*
魚膠 ,yü ,chiau, *isinglass.*
皮膠 .p‘i ,chiau, *glue.*
籐黃 .t‘eng .hwang, *gamboge.*
栲皮 'k‘au .p‘i, *mangrove bark.*
沙籐 ,sha .t‘eng, *rattans.*

15. Imported Wood.

烏木 ,wu muh‘, *ebony.*
重木桅 chung‘ muh‘ .wei, *masts and spars; hard wood.*
輕木桅 ,c‘hing muh‘ .wei, *masts and spars; soft wood.*
重木梁 chung‘ muh‘ .liang, *beams; hard wood.*
重木板 chung‘ muh‘ 'pan, *planks; hard wood.*
輕木板 ,c‘hing muh‘ 'pan, *planks; soft wood.*
麻栗樹板 .ma lih‘ shu‘ 'pan, *teak planks.*
紅木 .hung muh‘, *red-wood.*
毛柿 .mau shï‘, *camagon wood, or rough persimmon.*
呀嚂治木 ,ya .lan chï‘ muh‘, *kranjee wood.*

16. Imported Time pieces Telescopes etc.

自鳴鐘 tsï‘ .ming ,chung, *clocks.*
時辰表 .shï .c‘hen 'piau, *watches.*
珠邊時辰表 ,chu ,pien .shï .c‘hen 'piau, *watches, émaillés à perles.*
千里鏡 ,t‘sien 'li ching‘, *telescope.*
雙眼千里鏡 ,shwang 'yen ,t‘sien 'li ching‘, *opera glass.*
掛鏡 kwa‘ ching‘, *hanging mirror.*
穿衣鏡 ,c‘hwen ,i ching‘, *dressing glass.*

八音琴 ,pah ,yin .c'hin, *musical box.*

17. *Imported Cotton Goods.*

布疋花幔 pu' 'p'ih ,hwa man', *cotton and piece goods, printed and plain.*
棉花 .mien ,hwa, *cotton.*
原色布 .yuen 'saih pu', *grey shirtings.*
白色布 .paih 'saih pu', *white shirtings.*
無花布 .wu ,hwa pu', *plain stuffs.*
斜紋布 .sie .wen pu', *twilled stuffs.*
有花色布 'yeu ,hwa 'saih pu', *figured coloured cottons.*
無花色布 .wu ,hwa 'saih pu', *plain coloured cottons.*
花布 ,hwa pu', *fancy cottons.*
白提布 .paih .t'i pu', *white brocades.*
白點布 .paih 'tien pu', *white spotted shirtings.*
印花布 yin' ,hwa pu', *printed cottons.*
袈裟布 chia' ,sha pu', *cambric.*
洋紗 .yang ,sha, *muslin.*
緞布 twan' pu', *damask.*
柳條布 .lieu .t'iau pu', *dimities.*
各色毛布 koh' 'saih .mau pu', *ginghams, different coloured.*
麻棉帆布 .ma .mien .fan pu', *cotton and canvas duck.*
棉線 .mien ,sien', *cotton thread.*
棉紗 .mien ,sha, *cotton yarn.*
細蔴布 si' .ma pu', *fine linen.*
粗蔴布 ,t'su .ma pu', *coarse linen.*
回絨 .hwei .jung, *fustians.*
羽布 'yü pu', *bunting.*

18. *Imported Silk articles.*

手帕 'sheu .p'a, *handkerchiefs.*
眞金線 ,chen ,chin sien', *gold thread, real.*
假金線 'chia ,chin sien', *gold thread, imitated.*
眞銀線 ,chin .yin sien' *silver thread, real.*
假銀線 'chia .yin sien', *silver thread, imitated.*
哆囉呢 ,to .lo .ni, *broad cloth; Spanish stripes.*

嗶嘰 pi‘ ,chi, *long ells.*
荷蘭羽緞 .ho .lan ’yü twan‘, *Dutch camlets.*
英國羽紗 .ying .kwoh ’yü ,sha, *English camlets.*
羽綢 ’yü .c‘heu, *bombazeltes.*
小呢 ’siau .ni, *cassimeres.*
絨線 .jung sien‘, *woollen yarn.*
床氈 .c‘hwang ,chan, *blankets.*
花剪絨 ,hwa ’tsien .jung, *velveteens.*
羽綾 ’yü .ling, *lasting.*
小羽綾 ’siau ’yü .ling, *imitation lasting,* and *orleans lasting.*
剪絨 ’tsien .jung, *velvet.*

19. Imported Metals.

生銅 ,sheng .t‘ung, *unmanufactured copper.*
熟銅 .sheu .t‘ung, *manufactured copper.*
生鐵 ,sheng ’t‘ieh, *unmanufactured iron.*
熟鐵 .sheu ’t‘ieh, *manufactured iron.*
鉛塊 ,c‘hien k‘wai‘, *lead in pigs.*
鋼 ,kang, *steel.*
錫 ,sih, *tin.*
馬口鐵 ’ma ’k‘eu ’t‘ieh, *tin plates.*
日本銅 jih‘ ’pen .t‘ung, *Japan copper.*
鉛片 ,c‘hien p‘ien‘, *lead in sheets.*
白鉛 ,paih ,c‘hien, *spelter.*
黃銅釘 .hwang .t‘ung ,ting, *brass nails.*
商船壓載鐵 ,shang .c‘hwen .yah tsai‘ ’t‘ieh, *kentledge.*
鐵絲 ’t‘ieh ,sī, *iron wire.*

20. Imported Precious Stones, etc.

瑪瑙 .ma ’nau, *cornelians.*
瑪瑙珠 .ma ’nau ,chu, *cornelian beads.*
玳瑁 tai‘ mai‘, *tortoise shell.*
玳瑁碎 tai‘ mai‘ sui‘, *broken tortoise shell.*
玻璃片 ,po .li p‘ien‘, *window glass.*
珊瑚 ,shan .hu, *coral.*

21. Imported Animal Products.

牛角 .nieu 'chiau, buffalo horns.
生牛皮 ,sheng .nieu .p'i, raw buffalo hides.
熟牛皮 .sheu .nieu .p'i, tanned buffalo hides.
海龍皮 'hai .lung .p'i, sea-otter skin.
大狐狸皮 ta' .hu .li .p'i, large fox skins.
小狐狸皮 'siau .hu .li .p'i, small fox skins.
虎皮 'hu .p'i, tiger skins.
豹皮 pau' .p'i, leopard skins.
貂皮 ,tiau .p'i, marten skin.
獺皮 t'ah' .p'i, land-otter skin.
貉雚皮 .lauh ,hwan .p'i, racoon skin.
海騾皮 'hai lo' .p'i, beaver skin.
灰鼠皮 ,hwei 'shu .p'i, squirrel skin.
銀鼠皮 ,yin 'shu .p'i, ermine skin.
海馬牙 'hai 'ma .ya, sea-horse teeth.
整象牙 'cheng siang' .ya, whole elephants' teeth.
碎象牙 sui' siang' .ya, broken elephants' teeth.
兔皮 t'u' .p'i, hare skins.
麂皮 c'hi' .p'i, doe skin.
犀皮 ,si .p'i, rhinoceros skin.
翠毛 t'sui' .mau, king-fisher feathers.
孔雀毛 'k'ung 't'sioh .mau, peacock feathers.

22. Exported Oils, Wax, etc.

白礬 .paih .fan, alum.
青礬 ,t'sing .fan, green alum or copperas.
八角油 ,pah 'chiau .yeu, anniseed oil.
桂皮油 kwei' .p'i .yeu, cassia oil.
薄荷油 poh' .ho .yeu, peppermint oil.
牛油 .nieu .yeu, butter.
芝蔴油 ,chï .ma .yeu, sesamum oil.
桐油 .t'ung .yeu, oil of the dryandra tree.
荳油 'teu .yeu, bean oil.

柏油 cʻhieuʻ .yeu, *vegetable tallow.*
棉油 .mien .yeu, *cotton-seed oil.*
萆蔴油 piʻ .ma .yeu, *oil of palma-christi.*
白臘 .paih lahʻ, *bees' wax.*
茶葉 .cʻha yehʻ, *tea.*
八角 ,pah 'chiau, *star anniseed.*
麝香 shohʻ ,hiang, *musk.*
八角渣 ,pah 'chiau ,cha, *broken anniseed.*
時辰香 .shï .cʻhen ,hiang, *incense-sticks.*

23. *Exported Medicines.*

三奈 ,san naiʻ, *capoor cutchery.*
樟腦 ,chang 'nau, *camphor.*
信石 sinʻ .shïh, *arsenic.*
桂皮 kweiʻ .pʻi, *cassia lignea.*
桂子 kweiʻ 'tsï, *cassia buds.*
土茯苓 'tʻu .fuh .ling, *china root* (used for making biscuits).
澄茄 .cʻheng .cʻhiè, *cubebs.*
良薑 .liang ,chiang, *galangal.*
石黃 .shïh .hwang, *yellow lead* (massicot).
大黃 taʻ .hwang, *rhubarb.*
姜黃 ,chiang .hwang, *turmeric.*
上等高麗參 shangʻ 'teng ,kau .li shen, *best Corean ginseng.*
下等高麗參 hiaʻ 'teng ,kau .li shen, *inferior Corean ginseng.*
上等日本參 shangʻ 'teng jïhʻ 'pen shen, *best Japanese ginseng.* [*ginseng.*
下等日本參 hiaʻ 'teng jïhʻ 'pen shen, *inferior Japanese*
關東人參 ,kwan ,tung .jen shen, *Manchurian ginseng.*
嫩鹿茸 nenʻ luhʻ .jung, *young deer horns.*
老鹿茸 'lau luhʻ .jung, *old deer horns.*
中國牛黃 ,chung .kwoh .nieu .hwang, *Chinese cow bezoar.*
斑貓 ,pan .mau, *cantharides.*
桂枝 ,kwei ,chï, *cassia twigs.*
陳皮 .cʻhen .pʻi, *orange peel,* 橘皮 .chü .pʻi.

上等柚皮 shang' 'teng yeu' .p'i, *superior pumelo peel,*
（橘皮 .chü .p'i.）
下等柚皮 hia' 'teng yeu' .p'i, *inferior pumelo peel.*
薄荷葉 poh' .ho yèh', *peppermint leaf.*
甘草 ,kan 't'sau, *liquorice.*
石羔 .shïh ,kau, *ground gypsum; plaster of Paris.*
五棓子 'wu pei' 'tsï, *nut-galls.*
蜂蜜 ,feng mih', *honey.*

24. Exported Miscellaneous Articles.

料手鐲 liau' 'sheu .chuh, *bangles or glass armlets.*
竹器 .chuh c'hi', *bamboo ware.*
假珊瑚 'chia ,shan .hu, *false coral.*
爆竹 pau' .chuh, *fire-works* (formerly made of bamboo.)
羽扇 'yü shan', *feather fans.*
料器 liau' c'hi', *native glass ware.*
料珠 liau' ,chu, *native glass beads.*
雨傘 'yü san' *umbrellas.*
雲石 .yün .shïh, *marble slabs.*
通紙畫 ,t'ung 'chï hwa', *rice paper pictures,* (pith paper,)
（通草 ,t'ung 't'sau.)
紙扇 'chï shan', *paper fans.*
假珍珠 'chia .chen ,chu, *false pearls.*
古玩 'ku wan', *antiques; curiosities;* 古董 'ku 'tung.
細葵扇 si' .k'wei shan', *trimmed palm leaf fans.*
粗葵扇 .t'su .k'wei shan', *untrimmed palm leaf fans.*
駱駝毛 loh' t'o .mau, *camel's hair.*
棉羊毛 .mien .yang .mau, *wool.*
山羊毛 ,shan .yang .mau, *goat's hair.*
氈碎 ,chan sui', *felt cuttings,* or sui' ,chan.
紙花 'chï ,hwa, *paper flowers.*
土煤 't'u .mei, *Chinese coal.*

25. Exported Colours, Paper, etc.

銅箔 .t'ung .poh, *brass foil.*
紅丹 .hung ,tan, *red lead* (minium).
錫箔 ,sih .poh, *tin foil.*

銀硃 ,yin ,chu, *vermilion.*
油漆畫 .yeu ,t'sih hwa', *oil paintings.*
鉛粉 ,c'hien 'fen, *white lead* (ceruse).
黃丹 .hwang ,tan, *yellow lead* (massicot).
硃砂 ,chu ,sha, *cinnabar.*
上等紙 shang' 'teng 'chï, *superior paper.*
次等紙 t'sï 'teng 'chï, *inferior paper.*
油紙 .yeu 'chï, *oiled paper.*
墨 moh', *Indian ink.*
漆 ,t'sih, *paint.*
椶 ,tsung, *coir,* the thready bark of the tsung or coir tree.
蔴 .ma, *hemp.*
燈草 ,teng 't'sau, *lamp wicks.*
綠膠 lü' ,chiau, *green dye.*
廣東索 'kwang ,tung soh', *Canton twine hemp.*
蘇州索 ,su ,cheu soh', *Sucheu twine hemp.*
漆綠 ,t'sih lü', *green paint.*
礪殼 li' c'hiau', *oyster shells.*
綠皮 lü' .p'i, *green leather.*
土靛 't'u tien', *dry indigo.*
坑沙 ,k'eng ,sha, *manure cakes* or *poudrette.*

26. *Various Exported Ware.*

牛骨器 .nieu ,ku c'hi', *buffalo bone ware.*
牛角器 .nieu 'chiau c'hi', *buffalo horn ware.*
細磁器 si' .t'sï c'hi', *fine china ware.*
粗磁器 ,t'su .t'sï c'hi', *coarse china ware.*
白銅器 .paih .t'ung c'hi', *pewter ware.*
紅銅器 .hung .t'ung c'hi', *copper ware.*
木器 muh' c'hi', *wood ware.*
象牙器 siang' .ya c'hi', *ivory ware.*
漆器 ,c'hih c'hi', *lacquered ware.*
雲母殼器 .yün 'mu c'hiau' c'hi', *mother of pearl ware.*
籐器 .t'eng c'hi', *rattan ware.*

檀香器 .t'an ,hiang c'hi', sandal-wood ware.
金器 ,chin c'hi', gold ware.
銀器 .yin c'hi', silver ware.
玳瑁器 tai' mai' c'hi', tortoise-shell ware.
皮箱 .p'i ,siang, leather trunks.
皮槓 .p'i kang', leather boxes for holding silver.
皮器 .p'i c'hi', leather articles.
窰貨 .yau ho', earthen ware pottery.
黃銅器 .hwang .t'ung c'hi', brass ware.
銅鈕釦 .t'ung .nieu k'eu', brass buttons.
銅絲 .t'ung ,sï. brass wire.
生銅 ,sheng .t'ung, copper ore.
舊銅片 chieu' .t'ung p'ien', old sheathing copper.

27. Exported Wood.

竹竿 .chuh ,kan, bamboo poles.
籐肉 .t'eng jeu', split rattans.
椿梁舵柱 ,chwang .liang .t'o chu', piles, beams, cross-beams and pillars.
籐穰子 .t'eng .jang 'tsï, rattans stripped of bark.

28. Exported Clothing.

布衣服 pu' ,i .fuh, cotton clothing.
綢衣服 .c'heu ,i ,fuh, silk clothing.
皮靴緞靴 .p'i ,hiue twan' ,hiue, leather and satin boots.
皮鞋緞鞋 .p'i ,hiè twan' .hiai, leather and satin shoes.
草鞋 't'sau .hiè, straw shoes.
綢帽 .c'heu mau', silk caps.
氈帽 .chan mau', felt caps.
草帽辮 't'sau mau' ,pien, straw hat braid.

29. Native Linen and Cotton Manufactures.

細夏布 si' hia' pu', fine grass cloth.
粗夏布 ,t'su hia' pu', coarse grass cloth.
土布 't'u pu', native cotton cloth.
舊綿絮 chieu' .mien sü', old cotton rags.

綿被胎 .mien pei‘ ,t‘ai, *palampore or cotton bed quilts.*

30. *Exported Silk Manufactures.*

棉花 .mien ,hwa, *raw cotton.*
湖絲 .hu ,sï, *Hu-cheu silk.*
土絲 ’t‘u ,sï, *silk produced in the neighbourhood.*
絲經 ,sï ,ching, *thrown silk.*
野蠶絲 ’ye .t‘san ,sï, *wild raw silk.*
絲帶 ,sï tai‘, *silk ribbons.*
欄杆桂帶 .lan ,kan kwei‘ tai‘, *silk sashes with cassia flower pattern.*
絲線 ,sï sien‘, *silk thread.*
綢 .c‘heu, *pongees.*
緞 twan‘, *satin.*
絹 chiuen‘, *lutestring.*
縐紗 cheu‘ ,sha, *crape.*
綾 .ling, *damask silk.*
羅 .lo, *law, a kind of silk striped across with flowers.*
剪絨 ’tsien .jung, *velvet.*
繡貨 sieu‘ ho‘, *embroidered goods.*
絲綿雜貨 ,sï .mien .tsah ho‘, *silk and cotton mixtures.*
四川黃絲 sï‘ ,c‘huen .hwang‘,sï, *Sze-chuen yellow silk.*
同功絲 .t‘ung ,kung ,sï, *silk reeled from dupions.*
山東繭綢 ,shan ,tung ’chien .c‘heu, *Shan-tung silk piece goods.*
緯線 ’wei sien‘, *tassels.*
各省絨 koh‘ ’sheng .jung, *floss from various provinces.*
廣東絨 ’kwang ,tung .jung, *Canton floss.*
蠶繭 .t‘san ’chien, *cocoons.*
亂絲頭 lwan‘ ,sï .t‘eu, *refuse silk.*
各樣席子 koh‘ yang‘ .sih ’tsï, *matting.*
地席 ti‘ .sih, *mats.*
皮毯 ,pi ’t‘an, *skin rugs.*
氈毯 ,chan ’t‘an, *druggets and carpets.*

31. Exported Articles of Food, etc.

蜜餞糖菓 mih' chien' .t'ang 'kwo, *comfits and sweetmeats.*
醬油 tsiang' .yeu, *soy.*
白糖 .paih .t'ang, *white sugar.*
赤糖 ,c'hih .t'ang, *brown sugar.*
冰糖 ,ping .t'ang, *sugar candy.*
黃烟 .hwang ,yen, *tobacco.*
鼻烟 .pih ,yen, *snuff.*
烟絲 ,yen ,sï, *prepared tobacco in threads.*
烟葉 ,yen yeh', *tobacco in leaf.*
中國鼻烟 ,chung .kwoh .pih ,yen, *Chinese snuff.*
大頭菜 ta' .t'eu t'sai', *salted turnips.*
粉絲 'fen ,sï, *vermicelli* ('fen ,ser).
酒 'chieu, *samshoo.*
海菜 'hai t'sai', *seaweed.*
火腿 'hwo ,t'ui, *hams.*
鹹雞蛋 .hien ,chi tan', *salted fowl eggs.*
變蛋 pien' tan', *preserved duck eggs* (also 松花).
欖仁 'lan .jen, *olive seed* ('lan .jer).
橄欖 'kan 'lan, *olives.*
杏仁 hing' .jen, *apricot seeds or almonds.*
香菌 ,hiang hin', *mushrooms.*
金針菜 ,chin ,chen t'sai', *dried lily flowers.*
木耳 muh' .rï, *wood ear.*
桂圓 kwei' .yuen, *lung ngan, a fruit.*
桂圓肉 kwei' .yuen jeuh', *lung ngan, without the stone.*
荔枝 li' ,chï, *lichee, a fruit.*
蓮子 .lien 'tsï, *lotus nuts.*
芝蔴 ,chï .ma, *sesamum seed.*
落花生 loh' ,hwa ,sheng, or 長生果 .c'hang ,sheng 'kwo, *ground-nuts.*
花生餅 ,hwa ,sheng 'ping, *ground-nut cake.*
荳 teu', *beans;* 黑荳 ,heih teu', *black beans.*
荳餅 teu' 'ping, *bean cake.*
米麥雜糧 'mi maih' .tsah .liang, *rice, wheat and other cereals.*

蒜頭 swan‘ .t‘eu, *onions.*
栗子 lih‘ ’tsï, *chestnuts.*
黑棗 ,heih ’tsau, *black dates.*
紅棗 .hung ’tsau, *red dates.*

32. *Common Utensils.*

菜刀 t‘sai‘ ,tau, *chopping knife.*
麵杖 mien‘ chang‘, *paste roller,* or ’kan mien‘ kwun‘, *stick for*
筲箒 .t‘iau ’sau or .t‘iau ’shu, *straw brush.* [*kneading.*
担子 ’tan ’tsï, *brush made of* (,chi .mau) *fowl feathers.*
刷子 ,shwah ’tsï, *brush of pig bristles* (,chu .mau) *or goat's hair* (,shan .yang .mau). [*a pan.*
鍋 ,kwo, *iron cooking pan;* ,kwo ’ping, *bread cakes baked in*
飯勺 fan‘ .shau, *rice spoon;* ’ta ,kwo ’li .yau ,c‘huh fan‘ .lai, *take rice out of the pan.*
鏟子 ’t‘san ’tsï, *iron ladle;* ’t‘ièh tso‘ ,tih, *made of iron.*
碟子 .tièh ’tsï, *plate;* ,yih p‘eng‘ tsieu‘ p‘o‘, *with one blow*
碗 ’wan, *cup; basin;* fan‘ ’wan, *rice bowl.* [*it is broken.*
斧子 ’fu ’tsï, *axe or hatchet;* ,p‘ih .c‘hai, *to chop wood.*
面板 mien‘ ’pan, *kneading board.*
火爐 ’hwo .lu, *stove;* ,sheng ’hwo .lu, *light the stove.*
鎚 .t‘sui, *mallet;* .tsa ,tung ,si ,tih, *for beating things.*
釘子 ,ting ’tsï, *nails;* .lang .t‘eu, *hammer.*
鋸 chü‘, *saw;* chü‘ muh‘ .t‘eu yung‘ ,tih, *used for sawing wood.*
盆子 .p‘en ’tsï, *dish; basin;* ’k‘o ’i ’si ’lien, *for washing the face.*
瓶子 .p‘ing ’tsï, *bottle; jar;* .c‘heng .yeu, *to contain oil.*
廚櫃 .c‘hu kwei‘, *kitchen cupboard;* .c‘heng .tièh ’tsï ’wan, *to put away plates and basins.*
水壺 ’shui .hu, *kettle;* ,shau ,k‘ai ’shui, *to boil water.*
水筲 ’shui ,shau, *bucket;* ,t‘iau ’shui, *to carry water.*
雨傘 ’ü san‘, *umbrella;* ’tang ’ü yung‘ ,tih, *used to ward off*
茶壺 .c‘ha .hu, *tea-pot.* 叉子 ,c‘ha ’tsï, *fork.* [*rain.*
茶碗 .c‘ha ’wan, *tea-cup.* 調羹 .t‘iau ,keng, *spoon.*

33. *Vegetables.*

白菜 .paih t‘sai‘, *cabbage.*

生菜 ,sheng t'sai', *lettuce.*
薤菜 'chieu t'sai', *scallions.*
菠菜 ,po t'sai', *winter coarse greens.*
芹菜 .c'hin t'sai', *parsley.*
芫荽 .yuen ,sui, *caraway.*
蘿㽅 .lo peih', *turnips;* .hung .lo peih', *radishes.*
葱 ,t'sung *onions;* ,t'sung .t'eu, *onions bulbs.* [sant odour.
蒜 swan', *garlic;* 氣味不好 c'hi' wei' puh' 'hau, *unplea-*
山藥 ,shan yauh', *Chinese yam;* ,shan .yau .t'eu, *English*
荳角 teu' 'chiauh, *bean pods.* [*potatoes.*
香椿 ,hiang ,c'hun, *edible leaves of the* ,c'hun *tree.*
苦菜 'k'u t'sai', *sow thistle.*
蒲菜 .p'u t'sai', *spinach;* t'sui', *crisp.*
藕 'ngeu, *lotus roots;* 荷花 .ho ,hwa, *lotus.*
黃豆芽 .hwang teu' .ya, *yellow bean sprouts.*
綠豆菜 lüh' teu' t'sai', *green bean sprouts.*
西瓜 ,si ,kwa, *water melon;* .hu .lu, *gourd.*
王瓜 .wang ,kwa, *or* .hwang ,kwa, *cucumber.*
冬瓜 ,tung ,kwa, 倭瓜 ,wo ,kwa, *pumpkin.*
南瓜 .nan ,kwa, *or* .fan ,kwa, *flat yellow pumpkin.*

34. Domestic Animals.

鷄 ,chi, *fowl;* 鷄叫 ,chi chiau', *cock-crow.*
猫 .mau, *cat;* 拿老鼠 .na 'lau 'shu, *catch mice.*
狗 'keu, *dog;* 看家 k'an' ,chia, *watch the house.*
猪 ,chu, *pig;* 喂猪 wei' ,chu, *feed pigs.*
馬 'ma, *horse;* 備馬 pei' 'ma, *saddle a horse.*
牛 .nieu, *cow;* 耕地 ,ching ti', *plough the ground.*
羊 .yang, *sheep;* 放羊 fang' .yang, *let out sheep to graze.*
驢子 .lü 'tsï, *ass;* ,c'hien c'hü' ting' 'chang, *take him to be shod.*
騾子 lo' 'tsï, *mule;* pa' ,t'a t'au' shang', *put him in harness.*
鴨 ,yah, *duck;* 鴨蛋 ,yah tan', *duck eggs.*
鵝 .ngo, *goose;* 鵝毛 .ngo .mau, *goose quills.*

35. Birds.

燕子 yen' 'tsï, *swallow or martin.*

天鵝 ,t'ien .ugo, *swan.*
畫眉 hwa' .mei, *white-eyed thrush.*
野雞 'ye ,chi, *common pheasant.*
鳳凰 feng' .hwang, *phœnix.*
班鳩 ,pan ,chieu, *pigeon.*
鵪鶉 ,ngan ,c'hun, *quail.*
八哥 ,pah ,ko, *raven.*
老鴉 'lau ,kwa (read ,ya), *ringed raven.*
鷹 ,ying, *hawk.*
翡翠 ,fei t'sui', *variegated king-fisher.*
百靈 .paih .ling, *singing lark.*
喜鵲 'hi 'c'hüeh, *magpie.*
鸚哥 ,ying ,ko, *parrot.*
孔雀 'k'ung 'c'hüeh, *peacock.*
鴿子 ,koh 'tsï, *dove.*
野鴨 'ye ,yah, *drake.*
鴛鴦 ,yuen ,yang, *mandarin duck.*
魚鷹 .ü ,ying, *fish-hawk.*
杜鵑 tu' ,chüen, *goatsucker.*
大鴈 ta' yen', *wild goose.*
火雞 'hwo ,chi, *turkey.*
仙鶴 .sien .hauh, *crane.*
家雀 ,chia 'c'hüeh, *house sparrow.*
沙雞 ,sha ,chi, *grouse.*
扁嘴 'pien 'tsui, *broad-billed;* 尖嘴 ,tsien 'tsui, *sharp-billed.*
尾把老長 'i ,pa 'lau .c'hang, *long tailed.*
翅榜子大 c'hï' 'pang 'tsï ta', *its wings are large.*
掌不分綹 'chang puh' ,fen lieu', *web-footed.*
紅脖兒 .hung .poh .rï, *red necked.*
樹上 shu' shang', *on trees;* 打窩 ,ta ,wo, *make their nest.*

36. *Fishes.*

比目魚 'pi muh' .ü, *sole.*
沙魚 ,sha .ü, *shark.*

金魚 ,chin .ü, *gold fish.*
白鱔 .paih shan‘, *white eel.*
黃鱔 .hwang shan‘, *yellow eel.*
鯽魚 ’chi .ü, *bream.*
鯉魚 ’li .ü, *carp.*
鮎魚 .nien .ü, *silure.*
鯔魚 ’ti .ü, *mackerel.*
打魚網 ’ta .ü ’wang, *fishing net.*
釣魚鈎 tiau‘ .ü ,keu, *fish hook.*
玻璃魚缸 ,po .li .ü ,kang, *glass globe for gold fish.*
金魚池 ,chin .ü .c‘hï, *pond for gold fish.*
鮮魚 ,sien .ü, *fresh fish.*
鹹魚 .hien .ü, *salt fish.*

37. *Cart Furniture, etc.*

圍子 .wei ’tsï, *cloth covering of a cart.*
車簾子 ,c‘he .lien ’tsï, *cart blind.*
車輪 ,c‘he .lun, *cart wheels.*
車帳子 ,c‘he chang‘ ’tsï, *sun awning in front.*
車尾 ,c‘he ’wei, *projecting wood behind a cart.*
車轅子 ,c‘he .yuen ’tsï, *the shafts of a cart.*
鈎心 ,keu ,sin, *the part that connects the cart with the wheels.*
車箱子 ,c‘he ,siang ’tsï, *inside of a cart.*
籠頭 .lung .t‘eu, *horse collar.*
跨轅 k‘wa‘ .yuen, *to sit on the shaft.*
趕車 ’kan ,c‘he, *to drive a cart.*
騾子拉車 lo‘ ’tsï ,la ,c‘he, *mules draw the cart.*
開車 ,k‘ai ,c‘he, *to set a cart in motion.*
架轅騾子 chia‘ .yuen lo‘ ’tsï, *the shaft mule.*
邊套 ,pien t‘au‘, *the side mule, or leading mule.*
馬鞭子 ’ma pien‘ ’tsï, *whip.*
套車 t‘au‘ ,c‘he, *to harness a cart.*
車軸 ,c‘he .cheuh, *axle tree.*

38. Words used in Building.

砌墻 c'hi .t'siang, *to build a wall.*
抹泥 mo .ni, *to plaster with mud.*
麻刀 .ma ,tau, *hemp.*
方磚 ,fang ,chwen, *square bricks;* 'lei ,chwen, *build up bricks.*
白灰 .paih ,hwei, *lime;* ,shwah, *to brush.* [cement.
青灰 ,t'sing ,hwei, *blue lime; lime coloured to make a blue*
泥土 .ni 't'u, *mud; mortar;* tso' shang' ,ni, *put on mortar.*
攪草 'c'han 't'sau, *to mix straw.* [pavement).
石頭 .shïh .t'eu, *stone;* man' .shïh .t'eu, *place stones (as a*
木頭 muh' t'eu, *wood;* shang' .liang, *place beams.*
瓦 'wa, *tiles;* ,ngan shang' 'wa, *put on tiles.*
坯 ,p'i, *large earth-bricks;* 'lei ,p'i, *to pile mud bricks.*
葦子 .wei 'tsï, *reeds;* ,chiah .li ,pa, *to make a hedge.*
油漆 .yeu ,c'hih, *paint;* shang' ,c'hih, *to paint.*
截斷 ,chièh, twan', *a partition.*

39. Liquids.

酒 'tsieu, *wine; samshoo;* ,chen 'tsieu, *pour out wine.*
醋 t'su', *vinegar;* 'ta t'su', *buy vinegar.*
油 .yeu, *oil;* yih' ,chin .yeu, *a catty of oil.*
醬油 ,tsiang .yeu, *soy;* ,koh shang' .yeu, *put some soy in it.*
牛奶 .nieu 'nai, *cow's milk.*
黃酒 .hwang 'tsieu, *brown samshoo, made of coarse rice.*

40. Clothing.

袍子 .p'au 'tsï, *long robe with waist-band.*
綿襖 .mien 'ngau, *wadded gown without waist-band.*
砍肩 'k'an ,chien, *waist-coat.*
綿褲子 .mien k'u' 'tsï, *wadded trowsers;* t'au' k'u', *leggings.*
大褂 ta' kwa', *long summer robe.*
馬褂 'ma kwa', *jacket;* ,c'hwen shang', *to put it on.*
帽子 mau' 'tsï, *cap;* tai' shang', *to put it on.*
鞋 .hie, *shoes;* twan' .hie, *satin shoes.*
靴 .hiüe, *boots;* heu' 'ti 'tsï, *thick-soled.*
襪子 wah' 'tsï, *stockings;* ,tan wah' 'tsï, *single faced*
汗衫 han' ,shan, *shirt.* [stockings.
小褂 'siau kwa', *half summer robe.*

腰帶 ,yau tai‘, *girdle; waist band.*
扣子 k‘eu‘ ’tsï, *button;* ’nieu ’tsï, *button.*
領子 ’ling ’tsï, *collar.*

41. Sickness.

不爽快 puh‘ ’shwang k‘wai‘, *not in good spirits.*
不舒服 puh‘ ,shu ’fuh, *not well.*
腦袋痛 ’nau tai‘ .t‘eng, *head-ache.*
發燒 ,fah ,shau, *feverish.*
發瘧子 ,fah yauh‘ ’tsï, *ague.*
肚腹不好 tu‘ ,fuh puh‘ ’hau, *stomach out of order.*
長瘡 ’chang ,c‘hwang, *to have ulcers,*
發昏 ,fah ,hwen, *to faint.*
肉瘤子 jeuh‘ .lieu ’tsï, *wen.*
癱瘋 ,t‘an ,feng, *palsy.*
瞎子 ,hiah ’tsï, *blind man.*
發眼 ,fah ’yen, *inflamed eyes.*
灸瘡 ’chieu ,c‘hwang, *to foment.*
心跳 ,sin t‘iau‘, *palpitation of the heart.*
黄症 .hwang cheng‘, *jaundice.*
消化不動 ,siau hwa‘ puh‘ tung‘, *indigestion.*
發噁心 ,fah ,ngau ,sin, *tendency to vomit.*

42. Boat Furniture, etc.

風篷 ,feng .p‘eng, *a sail.*
運糧船 yün‘ .liang .c‘hwen, *grain junk.*
戰船 ,chan .c‘hwen, *war junk.*
攬渡 ’pai tu‘, *to ferry over.*
鹽船 .yen .c‘hwen, *salt boat.*
艙 ,t‘sang, *cabin; hold;* hia‘ ,t‘sang, *put down in the cabin.*
艙板 ,t‘sang ’pan, *deck planks.*
船桅 ,c‘hwen .wei, *mast.*
風信旗 ,feng sin‘ .c‘hi, *a streamer.*
桅燈 .wei ,teng, *mast lanthorn.*
跳板 t‘iau‘ ’pan, *shore plank.*
將軍柱 ,tsiang ,chiün chu‘, *posts on which ropes are wound.*

舵 to' *rudder,* 搬舵 pan to', *steer to the right.*
桅 .wei, *mast,* 推舵 t'ui to', *steer to the left.*
桅箍 .wei ,ku, *mast hoops.*
風鐶 ,feng .hwan rï, *ring for tackling.*
打號 'ta hau', *singing.*
頂風 'ting ,feng, *contrary wind.*
棹棹 tsau' tsau', *to row.*
拉篷 ,la ;p'eng, *raise the sail.*
船桿 .c'hwen 'kan, *path on side of boat.*
艙梯 ,t'sang ,t'i, *hatch way stairs.*
管船 'kwan .c'hwen ,rï, *chief boat-man.*
弄船 neng' .c'hwen, *to work the boat.*
撐船 ,t'seng .c'hwen, *the boat men.*
探繩 t'an' .sheng, *towing rope.*
官艙 ,kwan ,t'sang, *front cabin.*
火艙 'hwo ,t'sang, *cooking cabin.*
你們的船快像燕子似的 'ni ,men ,ti .c'hwen k'wai' siang' yen' ,tsï sï ,ti, *your boat is swift as a swallow.*
夥計都睡着 'hwo ,c'hi ,tu .shui .chau, *the boat-men are all asleep.*

43. *Furniture of a House.*

桌子 ,choh 'tsï, *table;* ,fang ,choh, *square table.*
椅子 'i 'tsï, *chair;* ,c'hiuen 'i, *round arm-chair.*
杌子 wuh' 'tsï, *stool;* yüeh' liang' ,choh, *round table.* [*two.*
板橙 'pan ,teng, *long stool; bench;* rï' .jen ,teng, *a stool for*
櫃 kwei', *cupboard;* 'ting ,siang kwei', *chest on the top of a cupboard.*
箱子 ,siang 'tsï, *chest;* .p'i ,siang, *leather trunk.*
被几 pei' ,chi, *a long table on which bedding is piled.*
茶几 .c'ha ,chi, *tea table.*
條案 .t'iau ngan', *long high table;* ,shu ngan', *table for* [*books.*
盆架 .p'en chia', *basin stand.*
書架 ,shu chia', *book-case;* ,koh ,shu ,tih, *for placing books.*
廚櫃 .c'hu kwei', *kitchen cupboard.* [*chest.*
行箱 .hing ,siang, *baggage trunk.* 茶箱 .c'ha ,siang, *tea*

花瓶 ,hwa .p'ing, *flower jar.* 花盆 ,hwa .p'en. *flower pot.*
鏡台 ching' ,t'ai, *mirror stand.*
貌鏡 man' ching', *looking glass.*
畫 hwa', *picture;* tsai' .t'siang shang' kwa' ,choh, *hung on*
對字 tui' 'tsï, *hanging sentences in pairs.* [*wall.*
脚踏 'chiau .ta, *foot-stool,* or .ta 'chiau ,teng, *the same.*
書箱 ,shu ,siang, *book box.*
讀書盤 .tuh ,shu .p'an, *a tray for pencils, inkstone, etc.*
木瓜盤 muh' ,kwa .p'an, *a tray on which is placed a fra-*
帽架 mau' chia', *hat stand.* [*grant melon.*
掛瓶 kwa' .p'ing, *a hanging jar;* 'k'o 'i ,c'ha ,hwar, *for*
飯桌 fan' ,choh, *dining table.* [*holding flowers.*
床 .c'hwang, *bedstead.*
燈 ,teng, *lamp;* kwa' ,teng, *hanging lanthorn.*

44. Insects, Reptiles, etc.

螞蟻 .ma ,i, *ant;* lan' .p'a, *crawling in disorder.*
臭虫 c'heu' .c'hung, *bug;* 'yau .jen, *they bite people.*
蜜蜂 mih' ,feng, *honey bee;* mih' ,feng ,wo, *bee-hive.*
蠹魚 tuh' .ü, *book worm;* ,c'hih ,shu, *eat books.*
蝴蝶 .hu ,t'ieh, *butterfly* (read .tie).
蜈蚣 .wu ,kung, *centipede;* 'yau .jen 'yeu .tuh, *they have a*
蚰蜒 yeu' .yen, *centipede with angular legs.* [*poisonous bite.*
蠶繭 .t'san 'chien, *chrysalis of the silk worm.*
蟬 .c'han or 螂蟧 ,chih .lieu, *cicada* or *broad locust.*
蟋蟀 ,sih shwai' or 蛐蛐 'c'hü 'c'hü, *cricket.*
竈王馬 tsau' .wang 'ma, *hearth cricket.*
蚯蚓 ,c'hieu 'yin or 蛐蟮 'c'hü shan', *earth worm.*
螢火虫 .yung 'ho .c'hung, *fire-fly.*
狗蚤 'keu tsau', *flea;* hwei' peng', *they jump.*
蒼蠅 ,t'sang ,ying, *house fly.*
螞蚱 .ma 'cha, 黃虫 .hwang .c'hung, *migratory locust.*
虱子 ,sï 'tsï, *louse.*
土狗 't'u 'keu, *mole cricket.*
蚊子 .wen 'tsï, *mosquito;* .wen chang', *mosquito net.*
蠍子 ,hieh 'tsï, *scorpion;* .na 'i ,pa ,choh .jen, *they sting with*
蠶 .t'san, *silk-worm;* 't'u .sï, *produce silk.* [*their tails.*

蛛蛛 ,chu ,chu, *field spider.*
五穀蟲 'wu ,kuh .c'hung, *weevil, corn-eater.*
蝦蟆 .ha ,ma, *toad.*
白翎 .paih .lier (.ling .rï) *sand-fly.*

45. Common verbs.

Abolish, 去 c'hü', 廢 fei'.
Accept, 收納 ,sheu nah'.
Add, 加 ,chia.
Affect, 感動 'kan tung'.
Amputate, 剌下 .la hia'.
Ascend, 上 shang'.
Ask, 問 wen' 要 yau', 請 't'sing.
Avoid, 免 mien', 避 pi'.
Baptize, 施洗 ,shï 'si.
Bathe, 洗澡 'si 'tsau.
Beat, 打 'ta.
Beat clothes, 捽 ,shwai.
Begin work, 動工 tung', kung.
Believe, 信 sin', 信服 sin'.fuh, 相信 ,siang sin'.
Bend, 彎 ,wan.
Besiege, 圍困 .wei k'wen'.
Bind, 綑綁 'k'wun 'pang.
Boil, 煮 'chu.
Bolt, 拴 'shwan.
Burn, 炒胡 'c'hau ,hu.
Bury, 埋葬 .mai tsang'.
Buy, 買 'mai.
Calculate, 筧 swan'.
Call, 招呼 ,chau hu'.
Call out, 嚷 .jang.
Can, 能 .neng, 得 .teh.
Carry, 帶 tai', 抱 ,pau.
Cease, 停 .t'ing, 止住 'chï chu'.
Choose, 揀選 'chien 'siuen.

Comply, 依從 ,i .t'sung.
Condemn, 定罪 ting' tsui'.
Confess, 認罪 jen' tsui'.
Congratulate, 恭喜 ,kung 'hi.
Connect, 接續 ,tsieh sü',
Conquer, 得勝 .teh sheng'.
Cough, 咳嗽 .k'o seu'.
Cover, 蓋上 kai' shang'.
Covet, 貪 ,t'an.
Crack, 裂開 lieh', ,k'ai.
Crush, 壓壞 yah' hwai'.
Cry, 叫 chiau', 喊 han'.
Cure, 治好 chï 'hau. ['chiau.
Cut, 剌 .la, *with scizzors,*
Decide, 定規 ting' ,kwei.
Delay, 擔擱 ,tan .koh.
Deliberate, 斟酌 ,chen ,choh.
Depend on, 倚賴 i' lai'.
Descend, 降下來 chiang' hia' .lai.
Desire, 願 yuen'.
Desist, 止往 'chï chu'.
Despair, 絕望 .tsiueh wang'.
Destroy, 毀壞 'hwei hwai'.
Detain, 留着 .lieu ,cho.
Die, 死 'sï, 去世 c'hü' shï'.
Differ, 差着 ,c'ha ,cho.
Diminish, 減少 'chien 'shau.
Direct, 指點 'chï 'tien.
Disclose, 露出來 lu' ,c'huh

.lai (also leu').
Discuss, 辯論 pien' lun'.
Disperse, 散開 san' ,k'ai.
Disregard, 不顧 .puh ku'.
Dissolve, 消化 ,siau hwa', 化 hwa'.
Distinguish, 分明 ,fen .ming.
Disturb, 攪動 'chiau tung'.
Divide, 分開 ,fen ,k'ai.
Divine, 占卜 ,chan puh'.
Do, 做 tso'.
Draw, 拉 ,la, 拖 ,t'o.
Drive, 趕 'kan.
Dry, 晒乾 shai' ,kan.
Dwell, 住 chu', 居住 ,chü chu'.
Eat, 吃 ,c'hïh.
Endure, 忍耐 jen' nai'.
Engrave, 刻字 ,k'eh tsï'.
Enjoy, 享受 'hiang sheu'.
Enquire, 打聽 ,ta ,t'ing.
Enter, 進去 tsin' c'hü'.
Entice, 引誘 'yin 'yeu.
Entrust, 託付 ,t'o fu'.
Escort, 護送 hu' sung'.
Examine, 考究 'k'au ,chieu.
Except, 除 .c'hu, 以外 'i wai'.
Exert yourself, 出力 ,c'huh lih'.
Expand, 伸寬 ,shen ,k'wan.
Extinguish, 滅沒 mieh' mu'.
Faint, 暈過去 ,hwun kwo' c'hü'.
Fall, 跌下 ,tieh hia', 掉下 tiau' hia'.
Fan, 打扇 'ta shan'.
Fear, 怕 p'a'.
Feed, 喂 wei'.

Feign, 假做 'chia tso'.
Fight, 打架 'ta chia'.
Finish, 做完 tso' .wan.
Fix, 定下 ting' hia'.
Flatter, 奉承 feng' .c'heng.
Fling, 擲 .jeng.
Flow, 流 .lieu.
Fly, 飛 ,fei.
Forbid, 禁止 chin' 'chï.
Forget, 忘 .wang.
Freeze, 凍冰 tung' ,pihg.
Fulfil, 成就 .c'heng tsieu'.
Gamble, 賭錢 'tu .t'sien.
Give, 送 sung'; 給 'chih ('kei).
Go, 去 c'hü', 往 'wang.
Grieve, 憂悶 ,yeu men'.
Guard, 把守 'pa 'sheu.
Guess, 猜 ,t'sai.
Help, 相幫 ,siang ,pang. 幫助 ,pang tsu'.
Hide, 藏匿 .t'sang nih'.
Hir, 租 ,tsu, 賃 lin'.
Imitate, 學 .hiöh, 效法 hiau' 'fah.
Imform, 告訴 kau' su'.
Injure, 傷害 ,shang hai', 損害 'sun hai'.
Instruct, 教訓 chiau' hiün'.
Intercept, 截攔 .tsieh .lan.
Investigate, 查察 .c'ha ,c'hah.
Invite, 請 't'sing.
Kneel, 跪 kwei'.
Tie a knot, 打結子 'ta ,chieh 'tsï.
Ladle, 鏟 't'san.
Lead, 引導 'yin tau'.
Leave it *there*, 留着 .lieu ,cho.

Leave a *place*, 離開 .li ,k'ai.
Lend, 借 tsie'.
Let, 出賃 ,c'huh lin'.
Lie down, 眠下 .mien hia',
躺下 't'ang hia'.
Lie (falsely), 謊話 'hwang hwa'.
Lift, 舉起 'chü 'c'hi, 擎起 .c'hing 'c'hi.
Look, 瞅 'c'heu, 看 k'an'.
Look after, 照應 chau' ,ying.
Make, 做 tso'.
Manage, 管理 'kwan 'li.
Mark, 打印 'ta yin'.
Match, 配着 p'ei' ,cho.
May, 可以 'k'o 'i.
Measure, 量 liang'.
Meet, 遇着 ü' ,cho.
Mend, 修 'sieu.
Mix, 調和 .t'iau .ho.
Mock, 戲弄 hi' leng'.
Molest, 難為 .nan .wei.
Nail, 釘 ting'.
Name, 起名 'c'hi .ming.
Obey, 遵從 .tsun .t'sung.
Offend, 干犯 ,kan fan'.
Oppose, 拒住 .chü chu'.
Ought, 應當 .ying ,tang.
Overturn, 推倒 ,t'ui 'tau.
Parch, 乾貼 ,kan ,t'ieh.
Peel, 剝皮 ,poh p'i.
Perforate, 穿過去 ,c'hwen kwo' c'hü'.
Perspire, 出汗 ,c'huh han'.
Plait, 打辮 'ta ,pien.
Plane, 刨 .p'au.

Pierce, 扎 ,chuh, 穿 ,c'hwen.
Plough, 耕 .keng or ,ching.
Pray, 禱告 'tau kau'.
Prepare, 預備 ü' pei'.
Print, 印 yin'. ['tseu.
Proceed, 上前走 shang' .t'sien
Produce, 出 ,c'huh, 生出 ,sheng ,c'huh. [cheng'.
Produce evidence, 引證 'yin
Prosper, 興旺 ,hing wang'.
Protect, 保佑 'pau yeu'.
Purify, 洗 'si.
Pursue, 追趕 ,chui 'kan.
Push, 推 ,t'ui.
Put, 擱 ,koh, 按 ,ngan, 放 fang'.
Rail at persons, 罵人 ma' .jen.
Reap, 收 ,sheu, 斂 'lien.
Read, 讀 .tuh.
Rebel, 造反 tsau' 'fan.
Receive, 受着 sheu' ,choh.
  do. 到手 tau' 'sheu.
Redeem, 贖 .shuh.
Redress grievances, 申寃 ,shen ,yuen.
Reduce, 減輕 'chien ,c'hing.
Refine, 煉 lien'.
Reform, 改正 'kai cheng'.
Release, 開釋 ,k'ai ,shïh.
Remove, 搬家 ,pan ,chia.
Repay, 賠還 p'ei .hwan.
Repent, 悔改 hwei' 'kai.
Reply, 回答 .hwei ,tah.
Represent, 當做 'tang tso'.
Reprove, 責備 tseh pei'.
Rest, 安息 ,ngan sih.
Return; 回去 .hwei c'hü'.

Reward, 賞 'shang.
Ride horses, 騎 .c'hi.
Rub, 磨 .mo.
Salute, 請安 'tsing ,ngan.
Scatter, 散開 san' ,k'ai.
Scoop, 挖 wah'.
See, 看見 k'an' chien'.
Seize, 拿着 .na ,cho.
Send, 打發 'ta ,fah, 稍信 ,shau sin'.
Serve, 事奉 shï' feng'.
Shake, 搖 .yau, 抖 'teu.
Shave, 剃 t'i'.
Shut, 關 ,kwan.
Sing, 唱 c'hang'.
Singe, 燒顏色 shau' .yen 'sai or seh.
Sit down, 坐下 tso' hia'.
Slap on the face, 打嘴巴子 'ta 'tsui pa' 'tsï.
Smear, 塗 .t'u, 噴 ,p'en.
Smile, 含笑 .han siau'.
Smuggle, 偷稅 ,t'eu shui'.
Snuff candle, 夾去蠟花 ,chiah c'hü lah' ,hwa.
Soothe, 安慰 ,ngan wei'.
Speak, 說話 ,shwoh hwa'.
Spend, 費用 fei' yung'.
Spin, 紡線 'fang sien'.
Sprinkle, 灑去 'sha c'hü'.
Start, 起身 'c'hi ,shen.
Sting, 刺 t'sï'.
Strike, 打 'ta.
Surrender, 投降 .t'eu .hiang.
Sustain, 當 'tang.
Swear, 發誓 ,fah shï'.

Take, 拿 .na, 取 't'sü.
Take up time, 耽誤 ,tan 'wu.
Taste, 嘗 .c'hang.
Teach, 教 chiau'.
Tear, 撕破 ,sï p'o'.
Tempt, 誘感 'yeu hwoh'.
Thank, 謝謝 sie' sie'.
Think, 思想 ,sï 'siang.
Thirst, 渴 'k'oh.
Throw, 擲 ,jeng.
Toast, 炕 k'ang', 烤 'k'au.
Translate, 繙譯 ,fan i'.
Treat, 看待 k'an' tai'.
Tremble, 發抖 ,fah 'teu, 打戰戰 'ta chan' chan'.
Try, 試試看 shï' shï' k'an'.
Turn back, 回轉 .hwei 'chwen.
Wait, 等候 'teng heu'.
Wake, 醒 'sing.
Waken, 叫醒 chiau' 'sing.
Warn, 警戒 'ching chie'.
Waste, 浪費 lang' fei'.
Watch the house, 看家 k'an' ,chia.
Weave, 織布 ,chïh pu'.
Weep, 哭 ,k'uh.
Weigh, 稱 c'heng'.
Wrap, 包着 ,pau ,choh.
Wring dry, 扭乾 'nieu ,kan.
Write, 寫 'sie.

46. *Distinctive Numeral Particles.**

個 ko‘, as in 一個人 .yih ko‘ .jen, *a man.* Also of cash, loaves, etc. [etc.
盞 ’chan, *small cup.* Used of lamps, tea-cups, china-trays,
張 ,chang, *to stretch.* Numeral of tables, bows, lips, etc.
隻 ,chïh. Numeral of fowls, sheep, boats.
枝 ,chï. Numeral of pencils, fifes, branches.
處 c‘hu‘, *place.* Numeral of places and houses.
封 ,feng, *to seal.* Numeral of letters and packets.
架 chia‘, *a support.* Numeral of cannon.
根 ,ken, *root.* Numeral of poles, masts, etc.
口 ’k‘eu, *mouth.* Numeral of coffins, bells, water vessels.
件 chien‘, *divide.* Numeral of things, clothes.
卷 chiuen‘, *roll up.* Numeral of pictures.
顆 ’k‘o, *small head.* Numeral of pearls and grain.
科 ,k‘o, *rank; order.* Numeral of trees.
管 ‘kwan, *pipe.* Numeral of fifes, pencils.
塊 k‘wai‘, *a piece of.* Numeral of dollars, stones, etc.
領 ’ling, *neck.* Numeral of mats, blinds, etc.
面 mien‘, *face.* Numeral of flags, drums, etc. ,c‘ha shang‘ .c‘hi ’tsï, *set up a flag.* [chairs.
把 ’pa, *handful.* Numeral of knives, mallets, clubs, spoons,
本 ’pen, *root.* Numeral of books, account books.
匹 ’p‘ih, *to pair.* Numeral of horses, mules, etc.
鋪 p‘u‘, *to spread out.* Numeral of beds and couches.
步 pu‘, *step.* Used of situations. Che‘ pu‘ .t‘ien ti‘, *such a position as this.*
所 ’so, *place.* Numeral of houses. [hundred cows.
頭 .t‘eu, *heap.* Used of aminals. ,San ’paih .t‘eu ,nieu, *three*
條 .t‘iau, *sprout branch.* Numeral of collars, clubs, ropes, dogs, dragons, snakes, fishes, roads, doctrines, etc.
頂 ’ting, *summit.* Numeral of hats, sedan chairs.
朶 ’to. Numeral of flowers.

---
* These particles are used to connect a number with its noun, when that noun represents an individual thing, i. e. when it is an appellative noun. There are about forty such particles, and of these arbitrary usage determines which shall be employed with any noun.

梁 to‘. Numeral of walls.
端 twan‘, *orderly.* Numeral of things, affairs.
座 tso‘, *a seat.* Numeral of inns, temples, hills, etc.
文 .wen. Numeral of copper cash.
尾 .wei, *tail.* Numeral of fishes.
位 wei‘, *seat.* Numeral of scholars, mandarins, teachers.

*Significant Numeratives.**

張 .chang, a *sheet of* paper, skin, flat thin cakes. 兩張竹紙
　'liang ,chang .chuh 'chï, *two sheets of bamboo paper.*
車 .c‘he, a *carriage load* or *barrow load* of wood, lime, bricks, etc.
折 .che, a *fold* of paper.
陣 chen‘, a *gust* or *burst* of wind, rain, hail (pau‘ 'tsï), or thunder. 打了一陣雷 'ta 'liau yih chen‘ .lei, *there*
棹 ,choh, a *table* of rice.　　　[*was a burst of thunder.*
炷 chu‘, a *stick of* incense.
船 .c‘hwen, a *boat load* of anything. 來了一船鹹魚
　.lai 'liau yih‘ .c‘hwen .hien .ü, *a boat of salt fish has come.*
幅子 ,fuh 'tsï, a *fold* of cloth, of blinds, of curtains.
封 .feng, a *sealed packet* of letters, etc.
項 'hiang, a *heap* of silver.
口 'k‘eu, a *mouthful* of rice, etc.
間 ,chien, an *apartment* of a house.
句 chü‘, a *sentence* of books, words.
塊 k‘wai‘, a *piece* of land, cake.
綑 .k‘wen, a *faggot* or *bundle* of wood, string.
溜 lieu‘, a *stream* or *tract* of water, land, etc.
粒 lih‘, a *grain* of corn, etc.
把 pa‘, a *handful* of rice, etc.
包 ,pau, a *bundle* of sugar, clothes, etc.
瓢 .p‘iau, a *scoop* of water, etc.　　　[of houses.
片 ,p‘ien, a *piece* of land, water, clouds, snow; a *collection*

---
* These words are used to connect numbers with material nouns or with other nouns, when a part of them needs to be spoken of. Significant numeratives are definite or indefinite. Those which are definite are weights and measures. Those which are indefinite are here exemplified.

篇 p'ien‘, a *piece* of writing or of a book.
疋 ‚p‘ih, a *piece* of cloth.
席 ₌sih, a mat, a feast, a *party* of guests.
扇 shan‘, a fan, *fold* of a door.
手 ‚sheu, a *hand* covered with blood, earth, etc.
手心 ‚sheu ₌sin, a *handful* of rice, etc.
擡 ₌t‘ai, a *load* (carried by two persons) of anything.
帶 tai‘, a *tract* of land, water, streets, clouds, etc.
擔 tan‘, a *load* (carried by one person) of anything.
道 tau‘, a *path* or *stream* of light.
頭 ₌t‘eu, a *head* or *end* of string.
挑 ‚t‘iau, a *load* (carried by one person).
條 ₌t‘iau, a *length* of anything.
帖 ₌t‘ieh, a *piece of* plaister, of gold leaf, etc.
點 ‘tien, a *dot*, a *little of*.
垛 ₌t‘o, a *heap* of salt, of cash; a *cake* of pastry, etc.
紽 t‘o, a *ball*, made by winding; a *cake* of pastry, etc.
頓 tun‘, a *meal of* rice, etc. a *beating* (with ‚ta, *to strike*.)
堆 ₌tui, a *heap of* earth, fruit, stones; *crowd* of men, animals.
團 t‘wan, anything round, a *ball* of hair, hemp, silk.
殘 ₌t‘san, a *meal*.   [cloth.
層 ₌t‘seng, a *story* of pagodas, towers; *thickness* of paper,
節 tsieh, a *joint* or *subdivision* of anything as of bamboo, a whip, a finger, the spine.
丸 ₌wan, a *pill* of medicine.
味 wei‘, *taste*, *kind*, of medicine, food, etc.

48. *Weights, Measures, Vessels, and other definite divisions.*

盞 ‘chan, small *cup*.
站 chan‘, a stage on a journey; in Kiang-nan 90 *li* or 30 English miles; in North China a distance varying between 60 and 130 *li*.
張 ‚chang *leaf* of a book, of paper, of gold leaf; a *single* skin.
章 ‚chang, *section* of a book.
丈 chang‘, *ten feet*, or 141 inches English.
抄 c‘haou‘, *the 1000th part* of a ‚sheng or *pint*.

秤 c'heng', 10 *catties'* or *pounds' weight*.
尺 'c'hïh, Chinese *foot*; 14 inches and one-tenth English.
橱 .c'hu, *a wardrobe; book-case.*
盅子 ,chung 'tsï, *a cup.*
分 ,fen, *a candareen* or *tenth part* of a mace; one cent; *tenth of* an inch; a minute.
毫 .hau, a small measure of length; *tenth* of a li.
下 hia', a stroke of the clock; an hour.
匣子 .hia 'tsï, *a small box.*
歇 hieh,會子 'hwei 'tsï, 會兒 'hwei .rï, ('hwur, in northern China,) *an instant of time.*
壺 .hu, *a tea pot* or *wine pot.*
忽 ,huh, 10*th part* of a hau.
斛 .huh, *five teu.*
日 .jïh', *day.*
缸 ,kang, a *large vessel* for holding water, and other liquids.
更 ,keng (,ching in the north), *a watch,* 5th part of a night; counted from night-fall to day-break.
刻 .k'eh, *quarter of an hour.*
斤 ,chin, *a catty,* or 1⅓ ℔. English.
傾 'c'hing, 100 meu of land.
角 'chiöh, *a drinking horn,* a *horn* of wine; 'chiauh, 4th of anything, corner.
卷 chiüen', *chapter* of a book.   [*handful.*
合 hoh', tenth of a sheng or pint; in northern usage, *a*
弓 ,kung, *a bow,* (as a measure for land) five feet.
句 chü', *a sentence.*
鑵 kwan', *a pitcher; a pot.*
筐子 ,k'wang 'tsï, *a basket.*
樞 kwei', *a wardrobe; cupboard.*
鍋 .kwoh, *a frying pan.*
籃 .lan, *a basket.*
簍 'leu, *a hamper* (with a small mouth).
里 'li, Chinese *mile,* ⅓rd of an English mile.
釐 .li, 10*th part* of a fen; 100th part of an inch.
兩 'liang, *a tael;* 1⅓ oz; sixteenth of a catty, or 1-12th of a ℔.

畝 'meu, 'mu, 240 *square pu'*, or 6,400 *square Chinese feet.*
秒 'miau, *a second.*
年 .nien, *a year.*
盤 .p'an, *a plate,* or tray of earthenware or wood.
盆 .p'en, *dish; bowl; basin.*
甓 peng', *an earthen pitcher.*
盃 ,pei, *a wine cup.*
瓢 p'iau, *a cocoa-nut scoop.*
瓶 .p'ing, *a bottle; vase.*
疋 'p'ih, 40 *feet of cloth.*
步 pu', *five feet,* used in measuring land.
煞 ,shah, *an instant* (southern).
晌 'shang, *a forenoon or afternoon.*
首 'sheu, *a piece of poetry.*
升 ,sheng, *a pint measure* (of rice 1½ catty in the north).
世 shï', *a generation; an age; thirty years.*
時 .shï, 時辰 .shï .c'hen, 時候 .shï heu', *an hour; two English hours.*
箱 .siang, *a chest; box.*
絲 ,sï, 100*th part of a* .hau; 10*th part of a* huh'.
歲 sui', *a year.*
筲 ,sau, *a bucket.*
代 tai', *a generation.*
口袋 'k'eu tai', *a bag.*
擔 tan', *a pecul; one hundred catties;* 133⅓ *English pounds.*
罈 .t'an, *a pitcher.*
趟 t'ang', *a column of characters.*
斗 'teu, *ten pints or sheng.*
牒子 .tieh 'tsï, *a plate.*
點鐘 'tien ,chung, *an hour.*
天 .t'ien, *a day.*
節氣 .tsieh c'hi', *solar term;* 24*th of a solar year.*
錢 .t'sien, *a mace; tenth of an ounce or tael* ('liang); *a piece of coined money.*
撮 ,t'soh, 100*th of a sheng or pint.*
寸 t'sun'. *a Chinese inch;* 1·175 *of an English inch.*

桶 'tʻung, *a barrel; cask* or *bucket.*
甕 wĕng', *a large water vessel.*
碗 'wan, *a small basin.*
葉 yeh', *a leaf* of a book.
月 yüèh', *a month.*

49. *Collectives.*

枝子 ,chï 'tsï, *a branch* of flowers, of a family, of an army.
串 cʻhwen', *a chain* of cash, beads, pearls.
副 fu', *a pair,* or *set* of antithetical sentences, of ear-rings.
行 .hang, *a rank* of trees, of parallel threads.
壺 .hu, *a quiver* of arrows.
夥 'hwo, *a company* of men.
軍 .chiün, *an army.*
塊兒 kʻwai' ,rï. the *whole* of a thing.
貫 kwan', *a chain* of gold, precious stones or pearls.
羣 .cʻhiün, *a flock* or herd of sheep, cattle, wolves.
股 'ku, *share* in trade, division of an army; *breeze of* wind.
排 .pʻai, *a raft* of timber, bamboo.
班 ,pan, *a set* of men; *rank* of soldiers.
片 pʻien', *a splinter; collection* of building.
雙 ,shwang, *a pair* of shoes, chopsticks (kʻwai' 'tsï).
帶 tai', *a tract* of land.
刀 ,tau, *parcel* of 100 or more sheets of paper.
套 tʻau', *a covering; cover* of books, (several stitched volumes placed together in a loose cover are called a tʻau.)
旗 .cʻhi, *banner.* 屬那一旗 .shuh 'na yih' .cʻhi, *to which banner does he belong?*
簇 .tsuh, *kindred.*
隊 tui', *a party* of five or more soldiers.
對 tui', *a pair.*

45. *Auxiliary Nouns of Quality.*

種 'chung, *sort* of men; *portion* of silver. 這種人 che' 'chung .jen. *this sort of men.*

項 hiang‘, *part of; sort of.* 這一項錢是僱船的那一項錢是僱車子的 che‘ .yih hiang‘ .t'sien shï‘ ku‘ .c'hwen ,tih,—na‘ .yih hiang‘ .t'sien shï‘ ku‘ ,c'he ’tsï ,tih, *this part of the money is to hire a boat, and that to hire a cart.* 這一項事情 che‘ .yih hiang‘ shï‘ .t'sing, *this sort of thing.*

杆 ,kan, *stem; sort of.* 他們又是一杆人 ,t'a ,men yeu‘ shï‘ yih‘ ,kan .jen, *they are another sort of people.*

類 lei‘, *sort of.* 不是一類的人 .puh shï‘ .yih lei‘ ,tih .jen, *he is not the same sort of man.*

般 .pan, *the same in kind, sort of;* 這般光景 che‘ ,pan ,kwang ’ching, *this sort of appearance.*

樣 yang‘, *kind of;* 這樣人品 che‘ yang‘ .jen ’p'in, *this kind of men.*

54. *Numeral Particles to Verbs.*

翻 ,fan, *to turn over.* 又是一翻來了 yeu‘ shï‘ yih· ,fan .lai ’liau, *he is come once more.*

下 hia‘, *numeral of strokes.* 打了三下鐘 ’ta ’liau ,san hia‘ ,chung, *it has struck three times.*

會子 hwei‘ ’tsï, *a meeting.* 去了一會子 c'hü‘ ’liau .yih hwei‘ ’tsï, *he has gone once.*

遍 pien‘, *to go completely round; numeral of seeing.* 瞧過兩遍 .t'siau kwo‘ ’liang ,pien, *I have looked through it twice.*

趟 t'ang‘, *a time; numeral of any action.*

遭 ,tsau, *numeral of revolutions; as of oxen grinding, the sun revolving.*

次 t'sï‘, *repetition; numeral of any action.*

55. *Phrases at an Inn* 店 tien‘.

乾净屋子 ,kan tsing‘ ,wu ,tsï, *a clean apartment.*
燒炕 ,shau k'ang‘, *light the brick couch.*
煮雞蛋 ’chu ,chi tan‘, *boil eggs.*
煎羊肉 ,tsien .yang jeu‘, *fry mutton.*
燉雞 tun‘ ,chi, *stew fowls.*

馬釘掌 'ma ting· 'chang, *shoe the horse.*
喂草料 wei' 't'sau liau', *feed him with straw and corn.*
牲口喂了 sheng 'k'eu wei' 'liau, *the animals are fed.*
房錢 .fang .t'sien, *money for lodging.*
打更的 'ta ,ching ,tih, *the watchman.*
炕上坐着 k'ang' shang' tso' ,cho, *sitting on the brick-bedplace.*
捆上鋪蓋 'k'wun shang' ,p'u kai', *tie up the bedding.*
鋪褥子 ,p'u juh' ,tsï, *spread out the mattrass.*
打開被 'ta ,k'ai pei', *unloose the coverlid.*
搠上垛子 ,sa shang' to' ,tsï, *pack the pack saddle.*
高粱豆子 ,kau .liang teu' ,tsï, *millet and beans.*

APPENDIX I.

Tones of the Peking dialect.

1. Words in the first tone class, 上平 shang p'ing, take the upper quick falling inflection; by the *falling inflection* being meant the tone of commands in English. But this becomes the upper even monotone, in combination with another word following. If a word of this class stands last without the accent, it assumes the lower quick even monotone, as in 外邊 wai' ,pien, *outside.*

2. Words in the second tone class, 上聲 shang sheng, take the lower quick or slow rising inflection. The rising inflection is in English the tone of questions. When two words of this class are placed together, the former takes the upper quick rising inflection, as in 洗臉 'si 'lien, *wash the face.*

3. Words in the third tone class, 去聲 c'hü sheng, take the lower quick falling inflection, or occasionally the lower slow falling circumflex, which first falls and afterwards rises. When two words of this class are placed together, the last is pitched high, and becomes the upper quick falling inflection.

4. Words in the fifth class, 下平 hia p'ing, take the upper quick rising inflection, or occasionally the upper quick

rising circumflex, which is a double inflection, first rising and then falling.

5. Words belonging primarily to the fourth tone class, 入聲 juh sheng, are, in the spoken dialect, distributed among the other tone-classes in the following manner:—

Old tone-class.	Initial letter.	Peking tone-class.
Upper juh sheng.	k, t, p, s. ts, ch, h, w, y.	Upper p'ing ,sheng 上平
Lower juh sheng.	k, t, p, s. ts, ch, h.	Lower p'ing sheng 下平
Lower juh sheng.	l, m, n. j, w, y.	去聲 c'hü sheng.

☞ This is the general law, but the exceptions are very numerous, and they admit, for the most part, of reduction to a few subordinate laws, which here follow, numbered 6 to 9.

6. Many upper juh sheng words, principally substantives, with the initials k, t, etc. and accustomed to be pronounced alone, are heard in the second tone or shang sheng,* e. g. 血 'hie, *blood*; 百 'pai, *a hundred*; 鐵 't'ieh, *iron*; 尺 'c'hï, *a foot*; 北 'pei, *north*; 塔 't'a, *a pagoda*; 脚 'chiau, *foot*; 筆 'pi, *pencil*. Many words whose usual tone is the first, take 上聲 shang sheng for a special sense, as 曲 ,c'hü, *crooked*, but 'c'hü, *a song*.

7. Words taken from the book language, and not used to be pronounced singly, or not themselves thoroughly colloquial, prefer the third tone or 去聲 c'hü sheng; e. g. 特 t'e, *purposely*; 確 c'hiüe, *true*; 朔 so, *new moon*; 設 shè, *to place*; 客 k'e, *a guest*; When a word has the first tone for a common colloquial sense, as 擱 ,ko, *to place*, it often prefers 去聲 c'hü sheng, for another sense it may bear in combination, as 躭擱 ,tan ko', *to remain anywhere for sometime*.

8. Certain syllables have a preference for the fifth tone, or

---

* Words needing to be pronounced singly would naturally adopt the second tone, which, in Peking, is enunciated with particular distinctness.

下平 hia p'ing, e. g. chu, chi, chï, fu, ko, tse, te, 福 fu, *happiness;* 得 teh, *to obtain,* etc.

9. The reading tone of many juh sheng words, which obey the preceding laws, is 去聲 c'hü sheng; and this is especially true of those that are colloquially attached to the first and fifth tone classes; all such, when used in poetry, are read with the intonation of c'hü sheng. In poetry, juh sheng words are all transferred to c'hü sheng, except a few found in shang sheng.

10. Words arrange themselves in groups of two, three and four, regulated by accent. The accent falls usually on the last word in a combination of two; on the second and fourth in a combination of four; and on the first and last in a combination of three. But when, as often occurs, two sounds are so closely combined as to become one dissyllabic word, the accent is on the first; e. g. 甚麼 .shen ,mo, *what?* 我們 'wo ,men, *we.*

11. When the accent is on the first of two sounds forming a dissyllabic word, or the one significant and the other enclitic, the last loses its proper tone, and assumes that of 上平 shang p'ing, the first tone class. This is the reason that the proper tone of the following, among many more common words, viz. 着 .cho, .chau, *it is so;* 兒 .rï, *son;* 門 .men, *door;* 頭 .t'eu, *head;* 麼 'mo, interrogative particle, 呢 .ni, interrogative particle, 子 .t'sï, *son,* 情 .t'sing, *thing;* 咯 lo, final particle; 爺 .ye, *father;* 來 .lai, *come;* 老 'lau, *old;* 個 ko', a particle, is in the Peking dialect habitually exchanged for 上平 shang p'ing, in certain familiar combinations; e. g.

留着 .lieu ,cho, *leave it there.*
衙門 .ya ,men, *mandarin office.*
裏頭 'li ,t'eu, *within.*
甚麼 .shen ,mo, *what.*
老子 'lau ,tsï, *father.*
事情 shï' ,t'sing, *thing.*
老爺 'lau ,ye, *aged sir;* a common title of address to mandarins.
回來 .hwei .lai, *come back.*
你老 'ni ,lau, *you my old friend.*

這個 che‘ ‚ko, *this*.

12. The initials k, t, p, ch, and ts, are always aspirated in the fifth tone-class, except when the words to which they belong are derived from 入聲 juh sheng.

13. The presence of the initials l, m, n, r, j, in the first tone-class, is limited to words which are exclusively colloquial, or affected in tone by the particular position of the accent, as explained in law 12.

14. The suffix 兒 ‚rï, attached to the substantives and other words very extensively in the north, is frequently absorbed into the word to which it is attached. The final letters n, ng, and the vowels are then exchanged for r, while the tone of the word is kept and that of the suffix is lost.

Normal form.	Colloquial form.	Observations.
人兒 ‚jen ‚rï	‚jer	e as in French *le*.
錢兒 ‚t‘sien ‚rï	‚t‘sier	e as in *mercy*.
餅兒 ’ping ‚rï	’pier	e as in *mercy*.
天兒 ‚t‘ien ‚rï	‚t‘ier	e as in *mercy*.
絲兒 ‚sï ‚rï	‚ser	e as in French *le*.
塊兒 k‘wai‘ ‚rï	k‘wair‘	----
鷄子兒 ‚chi ’tsï ‚rï	‚chi ’tser	e as in French *le*.
板兒 ’pan ‚rï	’par	a as in *art*.
風兒 ‚feng ‚rï (or ‚fung)	‚foer	e as in *mercy* as *for*

15. The words 一 i, *one*, and 不 pu, *not*, vary their tone according to their position in the collocation of words to which they belong. Before a word in 去聲 c‘hü sheng they prefer hia p‘ing. Before shang p‘ing, shang sheng, or hia p‘ing, they take the c‘hü sheng intonation, and when standing last they are heard in the first tone, e. g. 不是 ‚pu shï‘, *it is not so;* 不來 pu‘ ‚lai, *he did not come;* 初一 ‚c‘hu ‚i, *the first day of the month.*

Observations.

These laws serve for Tientsin as well as Peking, except that the first tone-class receives the lower slow even tone, and the third or c'hü sheng, the upper quick falling inflection.

In the distribution of the juh sheng words among the other tone-classes, there is little difference between the usage of Peking and Tientsin.

The student is recommended to verify these fifteen laws, with the aid of a native and Mr. Wade's very useful Peking syllabary. The tones there assigned to juh sheng words will be found to be, in many instances, irregular and uncertain. This is on account of the transition state of these words. Thus, 極, 夕, 習, chi, si, si, belonging to 下入 hia juh, should be in 下平 hia p'ing by law 5. But they are placed in the syllabary under 上平 shang p'ing. A Pekinese whom I consulted transferred them at once to 下平 hia p'ing. In such cases, the difference of authorities indicates that a transition is taken place, and the law of change tells us which sound will ultimately prevail.

I am happy here to take the opportunity of referring to assistance, which I derived from suggestions by Mr. William Stronach in regard to some of the preceding laws.

II.

Tones of the Nanking dialect.

1. Words in the first tone class take for their distinctive intonation, the lower slow monotone, or sometimes the lower slow falling inflection, which consists of a slide of the voice downwards.

2. Words in the second tone class, 上聲 shang sheng, take the lower slow rising inflection, or to express the thing differently, in enunciating them the voice slides upwards.

3. Words in the class known as 去聲 c'hü sheng, take the quick falling inflection.

4. Words in the fourth class, or 入聲 juh sheng, are short in time.

5. Words in the fifth class, or 下平 hia p'ing, take the upper quick rising inflection.

III.

Tones at Chefoo (Fuh-shan hien) (Yen-t'ai).

1. Words in 上平 shang p'ing, the first tone take the lower slow rising inflection.
2. Words in the second tone-class 上聲 shang sheng, take the upper quick rising inflection.
3. The third class 去聲 ch'ü sheng, takes the upper quick falling inflection.
4. The class called 下平 hia p'ing, takes for its intonation the lower quick falling inflection.
5. Words of the fourth class or juh sheng are distributed principally among the second and fifth classes; those of the upper division, or 上入 shang juh, preferring shang sheng, while such as are in the lower division, 下入 hia juh, are usually found in 下平 hia p'ing.

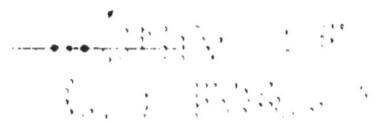

www.ingramcontent.com/pod-product-compliance
Lightning Source LLC
Chambersburg PA
CBHW020151170426
43199CB00010B/984